Cook Book

Recipes from Red Rock Country

by

Susan K. Bollin

GOLDEN WEST ☼ PUBLISHERS

Cover and interior art by Kris Steele

The author wishes to thank Joanne Goldwater and Carolyn Ross of Goldwater Foods of Arizona for the generous use of three of their recipes.

Library of Congress Cataloging-in-Publication Data

Bollin, Susan K.,
  Sedona Cook Book / by Susan K. Bollin
    p.   cm.
  Includes index.
  1. Cookery, American — Southwestern style. 2. Cookery —
    Arizona — Sedona.   I. Title
  TX715.2.S69B65   1994   94-12950
  641.5979—dc20   CIP

Some of the recipes contained herein were first published in *Salsa Lovers Cook Book, Quick-n-Easy Mexican Recipes* and *Chip and Dip Lovers Cook Book,* all by Susan K. Bollin and published by Golden West Publishers.

ISBN # 0-914846-98-1

Printed in the United States of America

Golden West Publishers, Inc.
4113 N. Longview Ave.
Phoenix, AZ 85014, USA
(602) 265-4392

Table of Contents

Appetizers

Breakfasts

Salads & Dressings

Salads (continued)

Soups & Chilis

Main Dishes

Main Dishes (continued)

Desserts (continued)

Beverages

Introduction

Sedona is famous worldwide for its magnificent natural beauty. Located in the central highlands of Arizona, approximately 120 miles north of Phoenix, Sedona is most famous for its spectacular red rocks. Sedona has also become a mecca for artists and writers, lovers of wildlife and especially for retirees from harsher environments. The Sedona climate is ideal; with its altitude of 4500 feet above sea level, all four seasons are represented at their best.

It is estimated that 15,000 cars a day pass through Sedona. And no wonder! Along with the incredible natural beauty, Sedona is also known for its resorts and restaurants. Enjoying the area's cuisine is one of the greatest pleasures of those living in or visiting Sedona. From simple to sophisticated, the influence of the southwest is apparent on every menu.

Sedona is famous around the world for its unusual red rocks, natural setting and spectacular scenery. But Sedona is also revered by many as one of the earth's sacred places. With the advent of the New Age movement, the area gained a new dimension. Many believe that a special energy emanates throughout the region. This energy relates to the earth's magnetic fields and is called a vortex. It is said that there are both positive and negative vortexes. A positive vortex extends energy and a negative vortex destroys energy. Believers feel that Sedona has more vortexes concentrated in the area than exists in any other place on earth. As a result of this concentration, special physical and psychic energies can be absorbed.

Native legends claim that early inhabitants of the region believed that the red rocks are the home of the Great Spirit and that this is a place of regeneration and of connection with the spirit world.

The author thanks those Sedonans who assisted with this book and hopes that this culinary guide through the red rocks will help keep the images of Sedona alive.

SEDONA

Appetizers

Rising majestically from the red rock mountains, the Chapel of the Holy Cross is a contemporary Catholic Shrine.

Sedona Red Chilequiles

Courtesy of Goldwater Foods of Arizona

1/2 bag (8 oz.) CORN TORTILLA CHIPS
2 cups SOUR CREAM
1 jar GOLDWATER'S® SEDONA RED SALSA
2 cups CHEDDAR CHEESE, shredded

Layer 1/2 of each ingredient, beginning with chips, in a medium baking dish. Repeat, ending with cheese. Bake in 350 degree oven for 30 minutes.

Serves 4 - 6.

For extra variety, try adding one or more of the following:

- **shredded chicken**
- **chopped onions**
- **jalapeños**
- **refried beans**

Supai Salsa Dip

2 cups creamed COTTAGE CHEESE
1 cup SALSA

Drain cottage cheese in colander. Place in small bowl. Stir in salsa and mix well. Serve with chips or crackers.

Makes 2 1/2 cups.

Queso Log

2 cups LONGHORN or medium CHEDDAR CHEESE, grated
2 cups MONTEREY JACK CHEESE, grated
1/4 cup MAYONNAISE (not salad dressing)
1/4 cup sour mash BOURBON
1/4 tsp. TABASCO® SAUCE
1 cup PECANS, crushed

Combine all ingredients until smooth. Shape into log and chill until set, about 2 hours.

 The first permanent resident in Oak Creek Canyon, John James Thompson, arrived in 1876.

Nachos

Nachos are a wonderful creation. They can be made as an appetizer, a snack or a meal and are an ideal way to use up leftovers.

Cover the bottom of baking pan with either corn or flour tortilla chips. Cover chips generously with grated cheese. Microwave or place under broiler until cheese is bubbly.

Some popular toppings:

- **green chiles**
- **jalapeños**
- **diced onions**
- **black olives**
- **chopped avocados**
- **diced meats**
- **beans**
- **diced tomatoes**
- **salsa**
- **sour cream**

Chipped Beef Roll-ups

1 jar (3 oz.) CHIPPED BEEF
1 pkg. (8 oz.) CREAM CHEESE
1 tsp. prepared HORSERADISH
1 tsp. dried PARSLEY FLAKES

Remove beef from jar and separate individual pieces. In small bowl, stir softened cream cheese, horseradish and parsley together. Spread thin layer of cream cheese mixture on each piece of beef, roll up tightly and fasten with toothpick.

Variations: Substitute **1 tsp. DILLWEED** for parsley

Makes about 1 dozen roll-ups.

The buff-colored Coconino sandstone forms the top layer of the red rocks. The sandstone that creates the striking red color is called the Supai formation.

Patio Paté

3 oz. CREAM CHEESE
1/4 lb. BRAUNSWEIGER
1/4 cup WHIPPING CREAM
1/4 tsp. NUTMEG
1/4 cup MUSHROOMS, diced

Combine all ingredients in medium bowl. Let stand at room temperature for 1/2 hour before serving. Serve with crackers.

Makes 1 cup.

Red Cliffs Shrimp Dip

6 lg. cooked SHRIMP, diced
8 oz. CREAM CHEESE
1/2 cup CHILI SAUCE
1 tsp. HORSERADISH
1/2 tsp. dried CELERY LEAVES

Dice shrimp, set aside. In medium bowl, stir cream cheese to soften. Add chili sauce, horseradish and celery leaves and mix well. Stir in shrimp.

Makes 1 1/2 cups.

Quick Dip Guacamole

2 lg. AVOCADOS, mashed
1/2 cup SALSA
1 tsp. LEMON JUICE

Stir all the ingredients together. Serve at once. Makes about 2 cups.

Chile con Queso

8 oz. processed CHEESE, cubed
1 can (4 oz.) diced GREEN CHILES
sprinkle of ONION SALT

Place cheese in medium bowl and melt in microwave. When cheese is melted, stir in chiles and salt.

Makes 2 cups.

Traditional Guacamole

2 lg. ripe AVOCADOS, mashed
1 sm. ONION, diced
1 lg. or 2 sm. TOMATOES, chopped
1 can (7 oz.) diced GREEN CHILES
1 GARLIC CLOVE, pressed
1 Tbsp. LIME JUICE

Combine all ingredients in small bowl. Serve at once. Makes about 2 cups.

 Sedona was founded in 1902 by a family of settlers named Schnebly. Mrs. Schnebly's name was Sedona and when her farmer husband opened a postal station, he named it for his wife.

Guacamole Spread

2 lg. or 3 med. AVOCADOS, mashed
2 pkgs. (3 oz.) CREAM CHEESE WITH PIMENTO
1 can (4 oz.) diced GREEN CHILES or 1 Tbsp.
    JALAPEÑOS, diced
1 Tbsp. ONION, minced
1 Tbsp. LIME or LEMON JUICE

Mix avocados and cream cheese together until completely blended. Add chiles, onion and juice. Cream together. Makes about 2 cups.

Cheese Crisp

Cheese crisps are one of the most popular appetizers and snacks of the Southwest. They are delicious plain or with toppings of choice added.

FLOUR TORTILLAS, any size
BUTTER or MARGARINE
CHEDDAR CHEESE, grated

Lightly butter tortilla on one side and broil until butter is lightly browned. Cover generously with cheese and broil until cheese melts and is bubbly.

Some additional toppings might be:

- **green chiles**
- **onions**
- **shredded meat**
- **black olives**

Frijole Dip

Frijole means bean in Spanish and is an important part of Mexican meals. Frijoles are so versatile that their uses in recipes are virtually unlimited.

1 can (16 oz.) PINTO BEANS, mashed
1 can (4 oz.) diced GREEN CHILES
1/4 cup MAYONNAISE
1/4 tsp. GARLIC SALT

Combine all ingredients in medium bowl and refrigerate until chilled. Serve with chips or crackers.

Makes about 2 cups.

Homemade Chips

1 pkg. CORN TORTILLAS
VEGETABLE OIL
SALT, if desired

Cut tortillas with scissors into quarters and fry in hot oil until crispy. Drain on paper towels. Salt if desired.

Makes about 4 dozen chips.

Quick Flour Tortillas

1 pkg. refrigerator BISCUITS
FLOUR, enough to lightly cover a small surface

Roll out biscuits on floured surface until very thin. Grill on hot frying pan or griddle until golden brown on each side.

Makes 10-12 depending upon brand used.

Cheese Spread

2 cups LONGHORN CHEESE, grated
1 cup SALSA
2 jars (4 oz. ea.) PIMENTOS, diced, drained
3 Tbsp. MAYONNAISE (not salad dressing)
1/8 tsp. fresh ground PEPPER

Combine all ingredients in medium bowl. Chill well.

Makes about 3 cups.

Breakfasts

Slide Rock State Park situated in Oak Creek Canyon, is home to a popular natural water slide and the historic Pendley Ranch House.

Baked Chile Rellenos for a Crowd

Perfect for breakfast and makes a great main dish, too!

4 cans (7 oz. ea.) diced GREEN CHILES
4 cups LONGHORN CHEESE, grated
    (or 2 cups longhorn and 2 cups Monterey Jack)
1 cup ONION, diced
2 Tbsp. dried CILANTRO leaves
1 tsp. GARLIC POWDER
1 Tbsp. LIME JUICE
4 EGGS
1 1/2 cups whole MILK
1 1/3 cups FLOUR

In large bowl, combine chiles, cheese, onion, cilantro, garlic powder and lime juice. Stir well and set aside. In medium bowl, beat eggs, add milk and flour and stir with whisk until mixture is smooth.

Lightly grease 13 x 9 baking dish. Fill with chile mixture, distributed evenly. Pour egg mixture over chile mixture.

Bake in 350 degree oven for 50 to 60 minutes or until casserole is golden brown. Allow to sit for 15 minutes after removing from oven. Cut into squares. Serves 12.

Note: Serve with salsa, sour cream and fresh diced cilantro, if desired.

Easy, Excelente, Enchilada Eggs

Sipapu Lodge Bed & Breakfast

3 FLOUR TORTILLAS
1 cup ENCHILADA SAUCE
1/2 cup COTTAGE CHEESE
1 cup CHEDDAR CHEESE, grated
6 EGGS
1/4 cup WATER
1/4 tsp. CUMIN
2 GREEN ONIONS, chopped
1 Tbsp. VEGETABLE OIL
GREEN OLIVES and PARSLEY, chopped

Cut tortillas into bite-sized pieces. Place in a large baking dish. Combine 1/2 cup of the enchilada sauce and cottage cheese and 1/2 cup of the cheddar cheese and heat in microwave 1 minute. Spread over tortillas. In medium bowl, combine eggs, water, cumin and onions and scramble in oil in medium skillet. Spread eggs evenly over tortilla mixture. Top with remaining 1/2 cup enchilada sauce and 1/2 cup cheddar cheese. Bake in hot oven long enough to melt the cheese. Garnish with olives and parsley.

Serves 6.

 Until the turn of the century, West Sedona was known as Grasshopper Flats! It was inhabited by thousands of grasshoppers which fishermen caught on their way to Oak Creek.

Whole Wheat Buttermilk Pancakes with Fruit

Cozy Cactus Bed & Breakfast Inn

1 cup BUTTERMILK
1 EGG
3 Tbsp. BUTTER or MARGARINE, melted
1/4 cup FLOUR, all purpose
1/2 cup FLOUR, whole wheat
1 tsp. BAKING SODA
fresh or frozen FRUIT, such as strawberries, blueberries or
  raspberries, allowing 1 tsp. per pancake.

Combine buttermilk, egg and butter in medium bowl. In separate bowl, stir together flours and baking soda. Combine with buttermilk mixture. Heat skillet or griddle to medium hot. Grease lightly and spoon 3 tablespoons of batter per pancake. When ready to turn, add 1 teaspoon of fruit to top of pancake. Turn and cook second side. Keep warm in 200 degree oven until ready to serve.

 Petroglyphs and pictographs are both abundant in the area. Petroglyphs, from Greek words meaning rock and carving, are pictures that have been carved into the rocks and are found in their original location of origin. Pictographs, from the Latin meaning literally picture ideas, are drawings on the rock surfaces.

Huevos por Brunch

1 lb. bulk CHORIZO
12 EGGS
1/2 cup MILK

Sauté chorizo in large frying pan until thoroughly cooked, breaking it up as it is cooking. Drain excess fat by placing cooked chorizo in colander and pressing out excess fat with spatula. Break eggs into medium bowl, beating with a whisk after adding every 2 eggs. When all eggs are added, stir in milk. Pour egg mixture in chorizo frying pan, heated to medium, wait 1 minute or until eggs begin to set. Add chorizo and cook until eggs are done. Serve at once.

Serves 6.

Cinnamon-Raisin Pancakes

1 cup MILK
1 EGG
1 Tbsp. VEGETABLE OIL
1 cup packaged PANCAKE MIX
1 tsp. ground CINNAMON

1/2 cup RAISINS
BUTTER or MARGARINE
MAPLE SYRUP or other
syrup of choice

Preheat a non-stick skillet over medium high heat. In a medium bowl, mix milk, egg and vegetable oil until well blended. Stir in pancake mix, cinnamon and raisins. Using about 1/4 cup batter, pour into skillet and cook until each side is lightly browned. Serve with butter or margarine and syrup.

Serves 2 with 4 medium pancakes each.

Oak Creek Eggs
Orchards Grill

VEGETABLE OIL
2 6-inch FLOUR TORTILLAS
2 oz. CHORIZO
2 EGGS
2 BLACK OLIVES
2 oz. (1/4 cup) CILANTRO HOLLANDAISE

Heat oil in deep heavy pot to 350 degrees. Drop in flour tortilla and push down with a 2 ounce ladle and cook until golden brown and holds the shape of a cup. Repeat with second tortilla. Cook chorizo and poach the eggs. Spoon half of the chorizo in each tortilla cup and place egg over chorizo. Ladle 1 ounce of hollandaise (see below) over each egg. Garnish each with a black olive and serve with home fries or hash browns.

Cilantro Hollandaise

2 EGG YOLKS
1 tsp. WATER
4 oz. (1/2 cup) clarified
   BUTTER
1/4 cup LEMON JUICE
dash TABASCO®

dash WORCESTERSHIRE
   SAUCE
1/4 bunch CILANTRO,
   chopped
1 tsp. WHITE WINE
pinch of GARLIC

Beat egg yolks with water, in a double boiler, over low heat until eggs become fluffy (do not let eggs stick to the bowl). Slowly drizzle in butter while beating rapidly. Stir in lemon, Tabasco, Worcestershire, cilantro, wine and garlic.

Serves 2.

French Toast Supreme

14 slices CINNAMON BREAD
1/2 cup BUTTER or MARGARINE, melted
4 whole EGGS
2 EGG YOLKS
1/2 cup SUGAR
4 cups HALF-AND-HALF (or 3 cups MILK and
    1 cup WHIPPING CREAM)
1 Tbsp. VANILLA
POWDERED SUGAR
3 cups fresh BERRIES or FRUIT

Brush both sides of bread with melted butter and place in buttered 9 x 13 pan. In large bowl, beat eggs and egg yolks together. Stir in sugar, milk mixture and vanilla. Pour mixture evenly over the bread slices. Bake in 350 degree oven for 25 minutes until tops are lightly browned. Cool on wire rack for 15 minutes. Cut into squares, sprinkle with powdered sugar and fruit.

Makes 4 servings.

Yavapai College and Coconino Community College provide a wide offering of courses in the Sedona area.

SEDONA

Salads & Dressings

The beautiful views, majestic mountains and refreshing climate inspire and attract visitors from all over the world.

Verde Salad

In Spanish, verde means "green"!

2 cups GREEN BEANS, cooked
1 cup PEAS, cooked
1/4 cup CELERY, chopped
1/4 cup ONION, chopped
1/2 cup BELL PEPPER, any color, chopped
1 jar (2 oz.) PIMENTO, diced
1/2 cup OLIVE OIL
1/2 cup SUGAR

Combine all ingredients and marinate in refrigerator for 8 hours or overnight. Serve well chilled.

Makes about 4 cups of salad.

 Montezuma Castle National Monument is 35 miles south of Sedona. It is one of the best preserved and oldest cliff dwellings in the Southwest.

Five Peaks Salad

1 cup canned FRUIT COCKTAIL
1 cup PINEAPPLE CHUNKS
1 cup ORANGE SECTIONS
1 cup SEEDLESS GRAPES
1 cup SOUR CREAM

Combine all five in medium bowl. Cover and refrigerate for 12 hours.

Serves 5.

Bean Salad

1 can (15 oz.) each PINTO BEANS, KIDNEY BEANS and
    BLACK BEANS, well drained.
1 can (7 oz.) diced GREEN CHILES, drained
4 GREEN ONIONS, cut in 1/4-inch pieces
1 cup LONGHORN or CHEDDAR CHEESE, grated
1 Tbsp. crushed RED PEPPERS
1 pt. (2 cups) SOUR CREAM

Combine all ingredients in large bowl. Refrigerate until well chilled.

Serves 4-6.

 Sedona averages 17 inches of rainfall per year.

Copper Cliffs Coleslaw

2 cups CABBAGE, shredded
1/4 tsp. SALT
1/2 cup VEGETABLE OIL
1/2 cup BASIL and GARLIC VINEGAR
1/4 cup MAYONNAISE (not salad dressing)
1 Tbsp. SUGAR
1 tsp. fresh GARLIC, squeezed

Combine all ingredients and mix well. Chill at least 1 hour.

This recipe makes about 6 salad servings. It is a wonderful addition to tacos in place of lettuce and is good to have available for impromptu occasions.

Tonto Salad

1 lb. can KIDNEY or NAVY BEANS, drained
2 cans (7 oz.) TUNA, water packed, drained
8 GREEN ONIONS, cut in 1/2-inch pieces
2 GARLIC CLOVES, crushed
1 cup OLIVE OIL
1/4 cup WHITE WINE VINEGAR
1/4 cup PARSLEY, chopped
1 Tbsp. CAPERS
1/4 tsp. ground ALLSPICE
LETTUCE leaves

In large bowl, combine all ingredients except lettuce leaves. Toss to blend and serve on lettuce leaves. This salad may be served chilled or warm.

Serves 6.

Pineapple Salad

1 cup SOUR CREAM
1/2 cup PINEAPPLE, crushed
1/2 cup shredded COCONUT
1 cup miniature MARSHMALLOWS
6 MARASCHINO CHERRIES, halved

Mix all ingredients in medium mixing bowl. Chill well.

Serves 3.

The Equal Salad

RED ONION, sliced thin
fresh MUSHROOMS, sliced
WATERCRESS
OLIVE or VEGETABLE OIL

salad VINEGAR
KETCHUP
SUGAR

In medium bowl, place equal amounts of onion, mushrooms and watercress, depending upon number of salads desired. In small bowl, mix equal amounts of oil, vinegar, ketchup and sugar, the amount depending on the size of the salad*. Add to salad and toss well.

* 1 cup of salad mixture = 1 Tbsp. each — oil, vinegar, ketchup and sugar.

Asparagus-Avocado Salad

1 bunch fresh ASPARAGUS, cooked
2 lg. AVOCADOS, cubed
1 Tbsp. LIME JUICE
1 lg. TOMATO, cubed
1/4 cup OLIVE OIL
1 1/2 Tbsp. BASIL VINEGAR
seasoned PEPPER to taste

Cut cooked asparagus into 1-inch pieces. Place in medium bowl, add remaining ingredients. Chill salad briefly and serve at once.

Serves 4.

Chile Salad

3 TOMATOES, chopped
1 lg. can sliced BLACK OLIVES, drained
6 GREEN ONIONS, cut in 1/2-inch pieces
1 can (7 oz.) whole GREEN CHILES, sliced
1 cup GARLIC CROUTONS
4 Tbsp. OLIVE OIL
2 Tbsp. WHITE WINE VINEGAR
LETTUCE leaves

Combine all ingredients and chill. Serve on lettuce leaves.

Serves 4.

Kaibab Potato Salad

2 lbs. NEW or RED POTATOES, cooked
2 Tbsp. fresh DILL, chopped
1/2 tsp. seasoned PEPPER
6 lg. GREEN ONIONS, cut in 1/4-inch pieces,
    including some tops
1/2 cup RADISHES, sliced
1/2 cup CUCUMBER, sliced
2 Tbsp. Dijon style MUSTARD
1 cup MAYONNAISE

Cut potatoes into bite-sized pieces. In large bowl, combine potatoes, dill, pepper, onions, radishes and cucumbers. Toss lightly. In small bowl, mix mustard and mayonnaise until blended. Add to potato mixture and stir. Chill well.

Serves 6.

Steak Salad

2 lbs. SIRLOIN or FILET STEAKS cut 1 1/2 - 2 inches thick
GARLIC SALT
PEPPER
1 stick (1/4 lb.) BUTTER
prepared GREEN SALAD for four

Grill steak over very hot coals, blackening both sides completely but leaving inside very rare. Remove steak to cutting board, slice very thin. Season with garlic salt and pepper. Melt butter in large skillet. Finish cooking steak in butter to desired doneness.

Place prepared salad in 4 individual bowls, top with steak slices.

Serves 4.

Sedona Shrimp Salad

1 lb. SHRIMP, cooked, deveined and peeled,
**   cut in bite-sized pieces**
1 CUCUMBER, peeled, sliced very thin
12 RADISHES, sliced thin
4 GREEN ONIONS, cut in 1/2 inch pieces
1/2 cup WHITE WINE VINEGAR
1 Tbsp. SUGAR

In medium bowl, combine all ingredients and toss well.

Serves 4.

Sauerkraut Salad

1 can or jar (16 oz.) SAUERKRAUT
1 cup CELERY, chopped
1 sm. RED ONION, sliced thin
1 GREEN PEPPER, seeded and diced
1 sm. jar (2 oz.) diced PIMENTOS
2/3 cup VINEGAR
1/2 cup VEGETABLE or OLIVE OIL
1 1/4 cup SUGAR

Drain sauerkraut and rinse under cold water. Drain well. In medium bowl, combine sauerkraut, celery, onion, pepper and pimentos. Toss well. In small bowl, blend vinegar, oil and sugar. Add to sauerkraut mixture and stir well. Cover and refrigerate all day or overnight.

Serves 4.

Black Bean Salad

1 can (15 oz.) BLACK BEANS, drained
3 EGGS, hard boiled, chopped
1/3 cup RED ONION, chopped
1/2 cup LONGHORN or MEDIUM CHEDDAR CHEESE, cubed
LETTUCE

Combine ingredients in medium bowl. When ready to serve, toss with salad dressing of choice. Serve on bed of lettuce.

Serves 4.

Roquefort Dressing

1 pint SOUR CREAM
1/4 cup MAYONNAISE
2 Tbsp. WHITE WINE VINEGAR
1/2 tsp. GARLIC POWDER
1/2 tsp. CELERY FLAKES
1 Tbsp. GRATED ONION
1/4 tsp. cracked PEPPER
1 cup ROQUEFORT® or BLEU CHEESE, crumbled

Combine all ingredients in medium bowl, omitting cheese. Chill thoroughly. Before serving, gently stir in cheese. Makes 3 cups dressing.

Note: Cheese is easier to use if it is thoroughly chilled before crumbling.

Southwest Seasoning

A wonderful southwestern flavor for salads and meats!

1/3 cup CHILI POWDER
2 Tbsp. each:
    dried CILANTRO LEAVES
    ground CUMIN
    dried OREGANO leaves
    dried SWEET BASIL leaves
1 Tbsp. GARLIC POWDER
1 Tbsp. dried THYME leaves

Combine all in medium bowl. Store in airtight jar in refrigerator for up to 4 months. Makes 1 cup seasoning.

SEDONA

Soups & Chilis

Oak Creek flows through Oak Creek Canyon. This watercourse provides spectacular scenery, recreational opportunities and peaceful solitude.

Tortilla & Chicken Soup

1 lg. WHITE ONION, chopped
1 can (7 oz.) diced GREEN CHILES, undrained
1 can (15 1/2 oz.) MEXICAN STYLE
    or STEWED TOMATOES
5 cups CHICKEN BROTH
4 cups cooked CHICKEN, diced
1 tsp. ground CUMIN
1/2 tsp. dried RED PEPPERS
2 tsp. WORCESTERSHIRE SAUCE
2 cups WHIPPING CREAM
3 lg. AVOCADOS, cubed
1 pkg. TORTILLA STRIPS

In large kettle, gently sauté onions and chiles. When onions are slightly limp, add all other ingredients except whipping cream, avocados and tortillas. Cover and simmer slowly for 1-2 hours. Turn off heat and stir in cream. Place avocado in 6 bowls, fill bowls with soup and sprinkle tops with tortilla strips.

Serves 6.

 Abraham James, Sedona's first settler is credited with naming Bell Rock, Steamboat Rock, Table Mountain and House Mountain.

Black Bean Soup

This is the easy way to a delicious treat. Serve this soup either hot or chilled.

Prepare **2 cans** of **BLACK BEAN SOUP** according to directions. Add **1/4 cup of DRY SHERRY** for each cup of soup. Top with thinly sliced fresh **LEMON**.

Camp Verde "Gazpacho"

This unique "soup" may be served warm, at room temperature or chilled, even though gazpacho, which means "vegetable soup," is usually served chilled.

8 med. RED POTATOES
1 med. ONION, sliced very thin
1 BELL PEPPER, seeded and diced
1 cup CARROTS, diced
1 tsp. GARLIC SALT
1 Tbsp. dried PARSLEY FLAKES
3/4 cup extra virgin OLIVE OIL
1/4 cup SWEET BASIL VINEGAR

Cook potatoes, cool and cut into cubes. In large bowl combine potatoes, onion, pepper, carrots, garlic salt and parsley flakes. In small bowl, mix olive oil and vinegar. Pour over potato mixture and toss gently. Serves 6.

Note: This distinctive gazpacho is especially nice served in a chilled sherbet glass.

Easy Western Chili

1 lb. ground BEEF
1 can (15 oz.) PINTO or BLACK BEANS, drained
1 med. ONION, chopped
1 can TOMATO PURÉE
1 GARLIC CLOVE, crushed
2 Tbsp. CHILI POWDER
1 tsp. ground CUMIN
1/4 tsp. ground ALLSPICE

Brown ground beef, drain any excess fat. Add remaining ingredients and simmer together for 15 minutes or longer, if desired. After preparation, the chili can also be kept warm in crockpot.

Serves 4.

Watercress Soup

Watercress grows in the streams of northern Arizona and is usually available in grocery stores.

1 pkg. CREAM OF LEEK SOUP MIX
4 cans (15 oz. ea.) CHICKEN BROTH
1/4 tsp. NUTMEG
2 cups CREAM
1 lg. bunch WATERCRESS, finely diced

Combine soup mix, broth and nutmeg. Simmer 15 minutes. Place 1 cup of the cream and 1/2 of watercress in blender or food processor and process until smooth. Add to soup along with remaining watercress. Simmer additional 10 minutes. Serve hot or chilled.

Serves 6-8.

Absolutely Perfect Arizona Chili

This superb chili has been a tradition of the Marshall family of Arizona for several generations. Here is the modernized version.

3 lbs. SIRLOIN, completely lean, cut into 1-inch cubes
1 lg. white ONION, chopped
2 lg. or 3 sm. BELL PEPPERS, chopped
1 can (6 oz.) TOMATO PASTE
1 tsp. ground CUMIN
1/2 tsp. OREGANO FLAKES
1 Tbsp. dried CILANTRO
1 can (7 oz.) diced GREEN CHILES
2 Tbsp. WHITE WINE VINEGAR
2 cans (14 1/2 oz. ea.) BEEF BROTH
1 Tbsp. white SUGAR
2 Tbsp. CHILI POWDER or to taste

Combine all ingredients in large kettle. Simmer on low for 10-12 hours or overnight.

Serves 8.

 Red Rock State Park is the newest in the Arizona Parks System. Its magnificent 286 acres abound with plants and wildlife. Traversed by Oak Creek and surrounded by red rocks, the park is home for over 150 species of birds and 450 species of plants.

Chili Verde

2 lbs. ground ROUND STEAK
4 cans (7 oz. ea.) diced GREEN CHILES, undrained
1/2 tsp. GARLIC POWDER
2 cans (15 oz. ea.) BEEF BROTH

Brown ground steak in large frying pan. When done, drain any excess fat. Return to pan, add remaining ingredients and simmer, covered, at least 4 hours or all day.

Serves 4.

 Zane Grey featured the Sedona area in many of his books.

Chicken Chili

1 lb. ground CHICKEN
1/2 cup ONION, diced
1 clove GARLIC, crushed
1/2 cup GREEN PEPPER, chopped
1 can (14 1/2 oz.) PINTO BEANS, rinsed and drained
1 can (15 oz.) TOMATOES
1 tsp. CHILI POWDER
1/4 tsp. OREGANO LEAVES
1/4 tsp. ALLSPICE
1/4 tsp. ground CUMIN

In a large skillet, brown chicken, onion, garlic and green pepper. Add remaining ingredients and stir well. Cover skillet and simmer over low heat for 1 1/2 hours.

Serves 4.

Corny Peanut Soup

3 Tbsp. BUTTER or MARGARINE
3/4 cup CELERY, diced
1/2 cup ONION, diced
1/2 cup chunky style PEANUT BUTTER
1 can (14 1/2 oz.) CHICKEN BROTH
1 pkg. (10 oz.) whole kernel frozen CORN
1 cup CREAM

In a large saucepan, melt butter over medium high heat. Add celery and onion. Sauté until tender and lightly browned. Stir in peanut butter and continue stirring until peanut butter is melted. Add chicken broth and corn and simmer gently for 15 minutes. Remove from heat, stir in cream. If necessary to reheat, use low heat.

Serves 4.

Posole

3 Tbsp. OLIVE OIL
1 med. white ONION, diced
1 tsp. GARLIC SALT
1 1/2 lb. ground PORK

1 tsp. ground CUMIN
1 tsp. ground OREGANO
1 can (15 oz.) HOMINY,
  undrained

Heat oil in large skillet. Add onion, garlic salt, ground meat, cumin and oregano. Sauté over medium heat until meat is thoroughly cooked and onions are lightly browned. Add hominy, cover skillet and simmer for 30 minutes. Serve in bowls with topping of choice such as sour cream, guacamole or tortilla strips.

Serves 6.

SEDONA

Main Dishes

(Continued next page)

Cathedral Rock is Sedona's most famous geologic formation. It is one of the most photographed sites in the United States.

Main Dishes — (Continued from previous page)

Pollo Limón
(Chicken with Lime)

8 CHICKEN breast halves
1 1/2 cups ITALIAN SALAD DRESSING
1 white ONION, sliced very thin
2 LIMES, sliced very thin

Coat chicken breasts with Italian dressing. Place in a single layer on baking dish or cookie sheet. Top with onion slices and then lime slices. Bake in 325 degree oven for 1 1/2 hours.

Serves 4.

Chicken Jalapeño

1 FRYER, cut into serving pieces
1 cup VEGETABLE OIL
1 lg. bag JALAPEÑO FLAVORED POTATO CHIPS, crushed

Pat chicken dry, set aside. Place oil in medium bowl. Add chicken and coat well. With a pin, puncture chip bag in several places and roll, using a rolling pin, to crush chips. Cut bag open, coat chicken with crushed chips. Line a cookie sheet with foil, dull side up. Place chicken on cookie sheet and bake in 350 degree oven for 1 hour. Serves 4-6.

Note: This recipe can be made with any flavored potato chips. It is especially delicious with barbecue flavored chips.

Ham with Tequila

2 lb. HAM slices, 1/4 inch thick approximately 1 lb. per slice
1/3 cup raspberry or other flavored MUSTARD
1/3 cup VEGETABLE OIL
1 can (15 oz.) TOMATOES WITH CHILES
1 can (12 oz.) MANDARIN ORANGE SLICES
1/3 cup TEQUILA

Coat ham slices with mustard and fry in oil. Slash edges to prevent curling. When well browned, remove from skillet and pour off any remaining oil. Return ham to skillet, add remaining ingredients, cover and simmer for 1 hour. Remove cover, increase heat and reduce any remaining liquid. Serve with pan drippings.

Serves 6.

Turkey Tortilla Bake

24 corn TORTILLAS
1/3 cup VEGETABLE OIL
3 cups TURKEY, cubed
1 can CREAM OF CHICKEN SOUP
1 can (7 oz.) diced GREEN CHILES
1 cup sharp CHEDDAR CHEESE, grated
20 PIMENTO STUFFED OLIVES, sliced

Dip each tortilla in hot oil for a few seconds to soften. Drain on paper towels. Layer 12 tortillas in bottom of medium baking dish. Layer with 1/2 of the turkey, soup, chiles and cheese. Repeat the layers. Top with the stuffed olives. Bake in 325 degree oven for 40-60 minutes.

Serves 6-8.

Apache Steak

2 lbs. sirloin STEAK
1/4 cup VEGETABLE OIL
1/2 tsp. CHILI POWDER
1 tsp. dried CILANTRO
1/2 tsp. dried OREGANO FLAKES

In small bowl, combine oil, chili powder, cilantro and oregano. Pour over steak. Broil steak to desired degree of doneness.

Serves 4-5.

Tequila Steaks

4 T-BONE or PORTERHOUSE STEAKS, about 12 oz. each
3 Tbsp. OLIVE OIL
1 Tbsp. seasoned PEPPER
1 tsp. GARLIC POWDER
2/3 cup TEQUILA

Trim fat from edge of steaks and slash edges in 2 or 3 places to prevent curling. In small bowl, combine oil, pepper, garlic powder and tequila. Marinate steaks in oil mixture for 1 hour, place on grill and use marinade for basting.

Serves 4.

Note: Bourbon may be substituted for tequila, if desired.

Tamale Pie

Tamale Pie leftovers are even better than the original!

Step 1:

2 lbs. lean GROUND BEEF
1 cup ONION, chopped
2 GARLIC CLOVES, pressed

Combine beef, onion and garlic and sauté until beef is cooked. Drain well and place in large bowl.

Step 2:

1 cup BEEF BOUILLON

Rinse beef pan with bouillon, scraping bits from bottom of pan. Add to beef mixture.

Step 3:

2 1/2 cups TOMATOES, fresh or canned
(and drained), chopped
1 can (15 oz.) whole kernel CORN, drained
1 tsp. dried CRUSHED RED PEPPERS
1 1/2 tsp. GROUND CHILI POWDER
1/4 cup OLIVE OIL
1 1/2 - 2 cups MASA (or corn meal), enough to
thicken mixture
2 cans (4 oz. ea.) sliced BLACK OLIVES
1 1/2 cup LONGHORN CHEESE, grated

Combine all the ingredients in Step 3 and add to beef mixture, reserving 1/2 the cheese to sprinkle on top.

Bake 1 hour in buttered, large casserole at 350 degrees. Let stand 20 minutes before serving. Garnish as desired.

Serves 8.

Rio Verde Chicken Enchiladas

From the collection of Goldwater Foods of Arizona.

VEGETABLE OIL
8 CORN TORTILLAS
2 whole CHICKEN breasts, cooked and shredded
1 cup ONION, chopped
3 Tbsp. PARMESAN CHEESE, grated
1 cup JACK CHEESE, shredded
1 jar GOLDWATER'S® RIO VERDE TOMATILLO SALSA
2 cups WHIPPING CREAM
4 EGGS
2 cups CHEDDAR CHEESE, shredded

Heat oil in medium skillet. Dip each tortilla in oil, frying quickly just until soft. In medium bowl, combine chicken, onion, parmesan and jack cheeses. Divide chicken mixture among 8 corn tortillas, placing mixture in center of each tortilla. Roll tortillas, tube style, and place seam side down in medium baking dish.

In medium bowl, blend salsa, whipping cream and eggs together well. Pour over tortillas, sprinkle with cheddar cheese. Bake in 350 degree oven for 30 minutes.

Serves 4 (2 enchiladas each).

Note: For a festive touch, garnish with guacamole, sour cream, shredded lettuce, chopped tomatoes, or chopped black olives. Try substituting spinach for the chicken and create a vegetarian delight!

Bisbee Loaf

From the collection of Goldwater Foods of Arizona and named for the famous Arizona mining town.

3 lbs. lean GROUND BEEF
1/2 lb. hot SAUSAGE, ground
1/2 red ONION, chopped
1/2 (12 oz.) jar GOLDWATER'S® BISBEE
    BARBEQUE-KETCHUP
1/4 cup Italian flavored BREAD CRUMBS
PEPPER to taste

Combine all ingredients in large bowl. Place in large loaf pan (or 3 small loaf pans) and bake in 350 degree oven for 45 minutes.

Serves 6.

Note: If desired, chopped carrots and bell peppers may be added to the loaf.

Barbecue Brisket

4-5 lb. BEEF BRISKET
1 cup MAYONNAISE
1 cup bottled CHILI SAUCE
2 Tbsp. WORCESTERSHIRE SAUCE
3 Tbsp. crushed RED PEPPER
GARLIC SALT to taste

Place brisket in large baking pan. In medium bowl, combine all other ingredients, pour over meat, cover tightly with foil and bake in 300 degree oven for 5-6 hours.

Serves 6-8.

Shrimp Jambalaya

A Southwestern version of this traditional favorite.

1 cup CELERY, sliced
2 cups BELL PEPPER, diced
2 med. ONIONS, sliced thin
4 Tbsp. BUTTER
2 GARLIC CLOVES, crushed
1 lb. cooked HAM, cubed
2 lbs. SHRIMP, deveined & peeled
1/2 tsp. TABASCO® sauce
1/2 tsp. CHILI POWDER
1 tsp. SUGAR
2 cans (15 oz. ea.) whole TOMATOES
3 cups cooked RICE

In a large dutch oven or skillet cook celery, bell pepper and onions in 2 tablespoons of the butter until limp but not browned. Add garlic and ham, cook another 5 minutes. Add remaining butter, shrimp, Tabasco sauce, chili powder and sugar. Continue cooking until shrimp are cooked and pink, stirring frequently. Add tomatoes and rice. Serve hot. Serves 8.

Southwestern Salmon

A quick and easy way to enjoy salmon

Place **SALMON** in single layer in glass baking dish. Top with **SALSA** of choice. Bake in 350 degree oven, uncovered, until salmon is thoroughly cooked but not dry.

Serve with lime wedges.

Baked Enchiladas

1 doz. corn TORTILLAS
1 Tbsp. VEGETABLE OIL
1 lg. white ONION, chopped
1 can (7 oz.) diced GREEN CHILES
4 cups cooked CHICKEN, cubed
4 cans CREAM OF CHICKEN SOUP
6 slices SWISS CHEESE

Place 6 tortillas in large, lightly greased, baking dish. Set aside. In medium skillet, heat oil and sauté onion and green chiles. Add chicken and soup and stir well. Pour half of chicken mixture over tortillas, layer remaining 6 tortillas and remainder of chicken. Arrange cheese slices over all. Bake in 350 degree oven for 30-45 minutes or until bubbly.

Serves 8.

Mexican Pizza

1 prepared PIZZA CRUST, uncooked
1 can (7 oz.) diced GREEN CHILES
1 cup SALSA
1 cup CHEDDAR CHEESE, grated
MEAT or CHICKEN topping, if desired

Place crust in pizza pan. Drain chiles and place on crust, pushing chiles into crust with back of fork. Bake pizza shell until almost done. Remove from oven, add salsa, cheese and meat. Bake until cheese melts.

Serves 4 (2 slices each).

Stuffed Pork Chops

2 Tbsp. ONION, diced
4 Tbsp. BUTTER or MARGARINE
1 cup BREAD CRUMBS
1/2 tsp. CHILI POWDER
4 Tbsp. MILK
6 lg. 1-inch thick PORK CHOPS with pocket slits
CHILE BUTTER, see below

Sauté onion in butter in medium saucepan over low heat. When onions are limp, add crumbs, chili powder and milk. Stir well. Stuff bread crumb mixture into chop pockets, secure with toothpicks. Arrange chops on broiler rack, baste with chile butter (see below) several times. Broil until thoroughly done.

Chile Butter

1 stick (1/4 lb.) BUTTER, melted
2 Tbsp. LEMON JUICE
1/2 tsp. GARLIC POWDER
1 tsp. ground RED CHILI POWDER

Melt butter in small saucepan. Add remaining ingredients and stir well.

Serves 6.

 The Grand Canyon, one of the seven wonders of the world, is only 110 miles northwest of Sedona.

Tacos de Pollo

The traditional taco is made with corn tortillas, however, "soft tacos" (made with flour tortillas) have recently become very popular.

1/2 cup VEGETABLE OIL
1 doz. CORN TORTILLAS, fried
2 cups cooked CHICKEN, diced
2 lg. TOMATOES, diced
2 cups CHEDDAR CHEESE, grated
2 cups LETTUCE, shredded

Heat oil in small skillet. Using tongs, dip tortillas one at a time (folded in half) into hot oil and fry until just crispy, about 5-10 seconds per side. Drain on paper towels. (Precooked taco shells are available in most markets.)

Fill with chicken, tomatoes, cheddar cheese and lettuce. Add salsa or taco sauce, if desired.

Other fillings could be beef, bean, vegetables or guacamole.

 Over 150 million years ago, prehistoric seas covered the Verde Valley, forming layers of sandstone, gravels and limestone. Many marine fossils can be found in the region.

Baked Lamb Chops

Long-standing feuds between cattle ranchers and sheep-herders once prevented much lamb from being served in the west. Fortunately, this dish is now here to stay.

8 LAMB CHOPS
1 Tbsp. GARLIC POWDER
1 Tbsp. dried ROSEMARY
2 cups medium dry WHITE WINE

Place chops in single layer in baking pan. Combine garlic and rosemary in small bowl and sprinkle equally over chops. Pour wine in pan. Bake at 375 degrees until done to desired degree, about 45 minutes for medium.

Serves 4.

Garlic Shrimp

1/2 lb. BUTTER, melted
2 Tbsp. OLIVE OIL
4 GARLIC CLOVES, pressed
2 Tbsp. fresh LIME JUICE
1/4 cup fresh CILANTRO, minced
2 lbs. lg. or 3 lb. med. cooked, deveined and shelled SHRIMP

In small saucepan, blend butter, oil, garlic, lime juice and cilantro and blend well. Arrange shrimp on plates, pour small amount of butter sauce in individual bowls for dipping shrimp.

Serves 6.

Carne Asada

This easy recipe is also ideal for crockpot cooking.

**2 lbs. TOP SIRLOIN or ROUND STEAK, cut into
    4 serving-size portions
1/2 tsp. dried CILANTRO
1/4 tsp. ground CUMIN
1/4 tsp. ground ALLSPICE
2 Tbsp. LIME JUICE
1 can (7 oz.) diced GREEN CHILES, undrained**

Place steak in baking dish or crockpot. In small bowl, combine all other ingredients and spread evenly over the steak. Bake in covered baking dish in 325 degree oven for 3-4 hours or cook for 8-10 hours on low setting in crockpot.

Serves 4.

Pollo Español

**4 boneless CHICKEN breasts
2 Tbsp. LIME JUICE
1 tsp. dried CILANTRO
1 tsp. CHILI POWDER
1 Tbsp. OLIVE OIL**

Place chicken in large skillet. In small bowl, combine remaining ingredients and pour over chicken. Cook, covered, over medium high heat for 30 minutes. Remove lid, turn chicken and continue cooking until chicken is done. Serve with pan drippings.

Serves 4.

Santa Cruz Chicken

3 Tbsp. VEGETABLE OIL
2 Tbsp. BUTTER
4 lbs. CHICKEN, cut into serving pieces
2 med. ONIONS, sliced thin
1 cup TOMATOES, chopped
1/2 cup fresh CILANTRO, minced
1/4 tsp. GARLIC PEPPER
1 1/2 cups CHICKEN BROTH
1/2 cup dry VERMOUTH
1 med. can MANDARIN ORANGES

Heat oil and butter and brown the chicken pieces in large skillet. When chicken is browned, remove and sauté onions in same pan until soft. Add tomatoes, cilantro, pepper, broth, vermouth and oranges. Return chicken pieces to skillet, cover tightly and simmer for 1 1/2 hours.

Serves 6.

Quesadillas

FLOUR TORTILLAS, any size
LONGHORN or CHEDDAR CHEESE, grated

Cover half of each tortilla with grated cheese. Fold tortilla in half and grill in hot frying pan on high for 1 minute. Turn over, pancake style, and grill other side. Cut into pie-shaped wedges.

Other fillings may be added to the quesadillas such as:

- diced chiles
- onions
- diced chicken
- ground beef

Spicy Pork Chops

3 Tbsp. VEGETABLE or OLIVE OIL
4 lg. PORK CHOPS
seasoned PEPPER to taste
1 tsp. ALLSPICE
1 can (15 oz.) sour CHERRIES, drained
1 cup sweet red WINE

Heat oil in large skillet. Brown chops on both sides. When browned, reduce heat, add pepper, allspice, cherries and wine. Cover and simmer approximately 1 hour or until chops are thoroughly cooked.

Serves 4.

Sherried Roast

4 lbs. BEEF ROAST, sirloin or tenderloin
4 Tbsp. BUTTER or MARGARINE, melted
1/2 cup ONION, diced
4 Tbsp. SOY SAUCE
1 1/2 cups SHERRY
1/4 tsp. GARLIC PEPPER

Bring roast to room temperature and place in roasting pan. In medium saucepan, melt butter. Add onion, soy sauce, sherry and pepper. Baste roast with sauce several times during cooking. Roast in 375 degree oven until desired degree of doneness.

Serves 8.

Broccoli with Shrimp Sauce

4 Tbsp. BUTTER or MARGARINE
4 Tbsp. FLOUR
1 1/2 cups MILK
1/4 tsp. LEMON PEEL
6 lg. or 10 med. SHRIMP, cooked, peeled and deveined,
    cut in bite-sized pieces
2 pkgs. frozen BROCCOLI SPEARS

Melt butter in medium skillet. Using a whisk, stir in flour. Gradually stir in milk, cooking until a medium sauce is formed. Stir in shrimp and lemon peel. Cook broccoli according to package directions. Drain broccoli in colander and place in serving bowl. Top with shrimp sauce.

Serves 6.

Minute Steaks Verde

4 minute STEAKS
FLOUR
VEGETABLE OIL
1 can (4 oz.) diced GREEN CHILES
1/2 cup CHEESE, grated

Flour steaks lightly, brown in hot oil. Transfer steaks to a baking dish, cover each with equal amounts of chiles and cheese. Microwave on high until cheese is bubbly.

Serves 4.

Cypress Chimichangas

A favorite of the Southwest, chimichangas are filled and rolled, or folded, tortillas which are baked or deep fried.

1 lb. GROUND BEEF
1 can (15 oz.) REFRIED BEANS
1/3 cup ONIONS, chopped
1 Tbsp. ground CHILI POWDER
1/4 tsp. GARLIC POWDER
1 can (7 oz.) diced GREEN CHILES
1 doz. FLOUR TORTILLAS, 10-12 inch size
2 cans (15 oz. ea.) TOMATO SAUCE
1 tsp. ground CUMIN
2 cups CHEDDAR CHEESE, grated

Sauté beef until cooked, drain well. Return to skillet and add beans, onions, chili powder, garlic powder and green chiles. Spoon equal amounts of beef mixture into center of each tortilla. Roll tortillas and place, seam side down, in large baking pan. Bake in 350 degree oven for 30 minutes. In medium saucepan, heat tomato sauce and cumin together. When chimichangas are done, top with tomato sauce and grated cheese.

Serves 6 (2 chimichangas per serving).

Basalt, rock resulting from ancient lava flows, is seen at the surface of many of the red rock formations. Massive columns of basalt are found near the head of Oak Creek Canyon.

British Enchiladas

An early visitor to Sedona, from Liverpool, fell in love with the area and never returned to England. Many local dishes reflect his British influence.

2 cups MASA
1 1/2 cups sharp CHEDDAR CHEESE, grated
1 Tbsp. BAKING POWDER
1 EGG
3/4 cup MASHED POTATOES (easiest to use instant)
WATER
1/2 cup VEGETABLE OIL

Combine all ingredients except water in large bowl. Add enough water to make firm dough. Let rest for 15 minutes. Form into thick (about 1/3 inch) round cakes and brown in oil. Drain on paper towels.

Serve with toppings and sauces of choice. Some suggestions are:

- salsa
- enchilada sauce
- green olives
- onions
- green chiles
- jalapeños
- black beans
- shredded lettuce

Approximately 30 miles southwest of Sedona is the famous mining town of Jerome. Now a converted ghost town, Jerome features interesting shops and stores, restaurants, inns and galleries.

Roasted Chicken with Wine

4 lbs. CHICKEN pieces
3/4 cup dry WHITE WINE
1/4 tsp. PAPRIKA
1/2 tsp. ROSEMARY, crushed

1/4 tsp. GARLIC POWDER
1/4 cup VEGETABLE or
  OLIVE OIL

Place chicken in single layer in roasting pan. In medium bowl, combine remaining basting ingredients. Baste chicken generously several times during cooking. Roast in 325 degree oven for 3 hours. If chicken browns too rapidly, cover loosely with foil until last 20 minutes of cooking. Serves 6.

Southwestern Cornish Game Hens

6 ROCK CORNISH GAME HENS, thawed if frozen,
  approximately 1 lb. each
1 jar (10 oz.) mild JALAPEÑO JELLY
8 Tbsp. (or 1 stick) BUTTER or MARGARINE

Wash hens and pat dry. Place birds, breast side up, in a baking pan. Set aside. In small saucepan, melt butter and jelly together. Place tablespoon of jelly mixture in cavity of each bird and generously brush the outside of each with mixture.

Bake in 350 degree oven for 1 1/2 hours basting frequently with jelly mixture. Serves 6.

Sedona Swordfish

4 1-inch SWORDFISH STEAKS
3 Tbsp. OLIVE OIL
2 tsp. dried BASIL
2 tsp. LEMON JUICE
2 GARLIC CLOVES, crushed

Place steaks on broiler pan. In small bowl, combine oil, basil, lemon juice and garlic. Brush on steaks. Broil until steaks are cooked.

Serves 4.

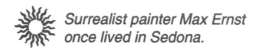 *Surrealist painter Max Ernst once lived in Sedona.*

Pineapple Spareribs

4 lbs. country style SPARERIBS
2 cans (15 oz.) TOMATO SAUCE
2 cans (8 oz.) crushed PINEAPPLE
2 Tbsp. LIQUID SMOKE
1/4 cup BOURBON
1/3 cup DARK BROWN SUGAR

Place ribs in large roaster. Combine other ingredients and pour over ribs. Cover tightly and bake in 325 degree oven for 1 1/2 hours. Remove cover, increase oven temperature to 425 degrees and roast another 30-45 minutes until ribs are browned.

Serves 6.

Sinagua Steaks

4 CUBED STEAKS
1 can (15 oz.) BLACK BEANS, drained
1/4 cup ONIONS, chopped
1/2 cup BARBECUE SAUCE

Sprinkle steaks with pepper, if desired. In small bowl, combine beans, onions and barbecue sauce. Place equal amounts of bean mixture on steaks, roll up and secure with wooden toothpicks or skewers. Brush with more barbecue sauce. Broil for approximately 15 minutes.

Serves 2-4.

Red Rock Chops

4 large PORK CHOPS
4 ORANGE SLICES
4 ONION SLICES
1/3 cup BROWN SUGAR
1/4 cup BOURBON

Arrange chops in single layer in baking pan. Place an orange and an onion slice on each chop. In small bowl, mix together brown sugar and bourbon. Pour mixture evenly over each chop. Bake in 350 degree oven approximately 1 hour or until chops are thoroughly done.

Serves 4.

Note: Be sure to try this recipe with chicken breasts instead of the chops!

Chicken Artichoke Casserole

3 lbs. CHICKEN breasts
SALT, PEPPER and PAPRIKA
6 Tbsp. BUTTER or MARGARINE
1 cup whole MUSHROOMS
1 can (15 oz.) ARTICHOKE HEARTS
3 Tbsp. FLOUR
2 cups CHICKEN BOUILLON
1/3 cup CREAM SHERRY

Sprinkle chicken with desired amount of salt, pepper and paprika. Place 4 tablespoons of butter or margarine in large skillet. Brown chicken. When all the chicken is browned, place in a 9 x 13 baking pan. Add mushrooms. Drain artichoke hearts and add to chicken and mushrooms in casserole. Add remaining 2 tablespoons of butter to skillet and melt over medium heat. Stir in flour until all flour is absorbed. Gradually add bouillon and continue stirring until thickened. Stir in sherry. Pour sauce over chicken, cover and bake in 375 degree oven for 45 minutes. Remove cover and bake an additional 30 minutes.

Serves 6.

 The Sinagua Indians built cliff dwellings in the area over 700 years ago.

Baked Chimichangas

12 - 12 inch FLOUR TORTILLAS
1 lb. ground ROUND STEAK
1 can (15 oz.) BLACK BEANS, drained
1 can (7 oz.) diced GREEN CHILES, undrained
1/4 cup GREEN ONIONS, sliced
1 can (4 oz.) sliced BLACK OLIVES, drained
LETTUCE
grated CHEESE
SALSA

Cook ground steak in skillet until thoroughly done. Drain if necessary and set aside. To skillet, add beans, chiles, onions and olives. Sauté lightly. Add beef and stir well. Spoon equal amounts of beef mixture onto each tortilla. Fold tortillas, envelope style, and place seam side down on baking sheet. Bake in 400 degree oven for 30 minutes. Serve with garnishes of lettuce, cheese and salsa.

Allow 2-3 per serving.

Oriental Chicken

2 lbs. CHICKEN breasts   **1/2 cup fresh LIME JUICE**
6 Tbsp. SOY SAUCE   **1/2 tsp. ground GINGER**
3 GARLIC CLOVES, crushed

Rinse chicken, pat dry and place in a nonmetallic baking pan. In small bowl, combine soy sauce, garlic, lime juice and ginger. Mix well, pour over chicken. Marinate several hours or overnight. Bake or grill until done.

Serves 4.

Judi's Chicken

Judi's Restaurant

6 boneless CHICKEN breasts
1 bunch fresh SPINACH, finely chopped
1 pkg. (8 oz.) CREAM CHEESE
1 Tbsp. cracked black PEPPER
1 tsp. GARLIC, minced
1 Tbsp. BASIL
1/2 cup BUTTER, melted
PUFF PASTRY DOUGH or PHYLLO SHEETS

Pound chicken breasts to flatten. Combine spinach, cream cheese, pepper, garlic and basil in large bowl (can be refrigerated until ready to use). Divide spinach mixture equally among chicken breasts. Fold chicken in half and drizzle with melted butter. Using your own puff pastry recipe or phyllo sheets, wrap chicken and brush with more melted butter.

Bake in 350 degree oven approximately 20 minutes or until golden brown.

Serves 6.

 You can take a railroad tour along the river and through the red rocks. The railroad begins in Clarkdale, a small town a few miles southwest of Sedona.

Paule á la Daniel

La Mediterranée Restaurant

4 CHICKEN breasts, boneless
1 bunch fresh SPINACH
1 cup MUSHROOMS, chopped
2 Tbsp. PINE NUTS
1 cup FETA CHEESE
dash SALT and PEPPER
1/2 cup WHITE WINE
SAUCE, if desired

Tenderize and flatten chicken between pieces of plastic wrap. Sauté spinach, mushrooms and pine nuts. Add cheese, salt and pepper and mix thoroughly. Divide filling between chicken breasts, roll and place in baking pan, pour wine over all. Cover with foil. Bake in 375 degree oven for 20 minutes. Remove from pan, slice diagonally 1 inch wide. Serve plain or with following sauce.

Sauce á la Daniel

1 GARLIC CLOVE, minced
1 cup MUSHROOMS, diced
1 cup heavy CREAM
1 tsp. GREEN PEPPERCORNS
dash SALT and WHITE PEPPER
1/4 cup WHITE WINE

Sauté garlic and mushrooms in wine. Add cream, peppercorns, salt and pepper. Simmer to reduce liquid. Pour over sliced stuffed chicken.

Serves 4.

Shrimp Quesadilla

L'Auberge de Sedona

4 (16-20 count) SHRIMP, peeled and deveined
1 GREEN CHILE, roasted, peeled, seeded and diced
1 Tbsp. CILANTRO
1 tsp. SOUTHWESTERN SPICE
2 Tbsp. BUTTER
1 (10-inch) FLOUR TORTILLA
3 oz. JACK and CHEDDAR CHEESE, shredded
    and mixed together
2 oz. SALSA

Cook shrimp in butter with green chile, cilantro and southwestern spice (see below). When cooked, dice shrimp. Heat 2 tablespoons of butter in large frying pan. Add flour tortilla. Sprinkle cheese and shrimp over half of tortilla. Fold over and turn. Cook until both sides are golden brown. Cut into 4 pieces. Serve with salsa and garnish with parsley.

Southwestern Spice

1/4 cup CHILI POWDER
4 tsp. ground CUMIN
1/2 Tbsp. ground OREGANO
1 tsp. ground BASIL

Combine in small bowl and stir well.

 Stick-Leg Gulch was named for a man who fell into a century plant that stuck in his leg.

Rummed Ham and Beans

2 cans (16 oz.) PORK AND BEANS
1 lb. cooked HAM, diced
1 sm. ONION, chopped
1 tsp. ground CLOVES
1 tsp. dry MUSTARD
1/4 cup DARK RUM

Place beans in medium baking dish, top with diced ham. In small bowl, mix together onions, cloves and mustard. Sprinkle evenly over ham and beans. Bake in 325 degree oven for 1 hour. Remove from oven, pour rum over all and bake an additional 15 minutes.

Serves 4-6.

Pork Chops in the Red

4 PORK CHOPS
1 can (15 oz.) ENCHILADA SAUCE
1 tsp. dried OREGANO
1 tsp. ground CUMIN
GARLIC POWDER to taste

Place pork chops in single layer in baking pan. Pour sauce over all. Sprinkle oregano, cumin and garlic powder evenly over chops. Cover tightly with foil and bake in 350 degree oven for 1 hour or until chops are thoroughly cooked. Serve with pan drippings spooned over each chop.

Allow 2 chops per person.

Roquefort Hamburgers

1 1/2 lbs. GROUND ROUND STEAK
1/3 cup ROQUEFORT® CHEESE
1/4 cup CREAM CHEESE
2 Tbsp. MAYONNAISE
1 tsp. WORCESTERSHIRE SAUCE

Shape ground round steak into 4 patties. Cook patties until done. In a small bowl, cream together both cheeses, mayonnaise and Worcestershire sauce. Top each patty with equal amounts of cheese mixture. Serve with or without buns.

Serves 4.

 Visitors to Sedona can enjoy an interesting shopping tour by hopping aboard the Sedona Trolley.

Herbed Chicken

1 cup VEGETABLE OIL
1/2 cup LIME JUICE
1/2 tsp. MARJORAM
1/2 tsp. OREGANO
1 tsp. dried CILANTRO
4 lbs. CHICKEN pieces

In small bowl, mix oil, lime juice and herbs. Brush over chicken. Broil chicken on medium rack in oven for approximately 30 minutes on each side.

Serves 4-6.

Plum Chicken

1 can (16 oz.) PLUMS, pitted
1 Tbsp. SOY SAUCE
2 Tbsp. VEGETABLE OIL
2 Tbsp. BROWN SUGAR
1/2 tsp. ground GINGER
8 CHICKEN breasts, halves or 4 whole

Combine plums, soy sauce, oil, sugar and ginger in blender or food processor. Blend until almost smooth. Place chicken in large baking pan, single layer and top with plum sauce. Cover with foil, dull side down, and bake in 350 degree oven for 1 hour. Remove foil and bake an additional 20-30 minutes.

Serves 4-6.

Kachina Chicken

1/2 lb. CHICKEN TENDERS
2 tsp. VEGETABLE OIL
1/4 cup light SOY SAUCE
1/4 cup CHICKEN BOUILLON
1/4 cup SHERRY
1 GARLIC CLOVE, crushed
1/2 tsp. ground GINGER
1 tsp. CORNSTARCH
1/4 tsp. dried crushed RED PEPPERS

Brown chicken in oil, remove from pan and set aside. In the same pan, combine all other ingredients and stir until slightly thickened, cooking over medium heat. Return chicken to pan and cook until done.

Serves 2.

Coconino Chicken

4 Tbsp. BUTTER or MARGARINE
2 lbs. boneless CHICKEN breasts
1/2 tsp. PAPRIKA
1/4 tsp. PEPPER
1 lg. can or jar MUSHROOMS, drained
2 Tbsp. BUTTER or MARGARINE
2 Tbsp. FLOUR
2 1/2 cups CHICKEN BROTH
1 jar (15 oz.) ARTICHOKE HEARTS, water packed
4 Tbsp. CREAM SHERRY

Melt 4 tablespoons butter or margarine in large skillet. Sprinkle chicken evenly with paprika and pepper and sauté in butter until well browned. Remove to lightly buttered baking dish. Add mushrooms to baking dish, covering chicken. Add 2 tablespoons butter to chicken skillet, stir in flour, add broth and cook until thickened. Remove from heat, add artichoke hearts and sherry. Pour over all in baking dish. Bake in 375 degree oven, covered, for 1 hour.

Serves 6.

Note: This delightful dish can be prepared a day or so in advance and baked as needed. Let casserole sit 1/2 hour after removing from refrigerator before baking.

 Devil's Dining Room: A sink hole originally called Devil's Kitchen until it caved in dramatically in 1880, filling the air with dust.

Supai Shrimp

3 Tbsp. BUTTER or MARGARINE
3 Tbsp. FLOUR
3/4 tsp. dry MUSTARD
fresh ground PEPPER to taste
1 cup HALF-AND-HALF
1/2 cup MILK
1 lb. SHRIMP, cooked, peeled and deveined,
    cut to bite-sized pieces
3 slices BREAD, cut into cubes
1/2 cup Italian flavored BREAD CRUMBS

Melt butter or margarine in large skillet. Stir in flour with a whisk until all flour is absorbed. Sprinkle in mustard and pepper. Slowly add the half-and-half and milk and cook until thickened. Add shrimp and bread cubes. Pour mixture into lightly buttered baking dish. Top with bread crumbs. Bake in 350 degree oven 30 minutes or until bubbly. Serves 4.

Pollo con Frijoles Negro

(Chicken with Black Beans)

2 whole or 4 half CHICKEN breasts, cooked
1 can (15 oz.) BLACK BEANS, drained
1/2 cup SALSA
1/2 cup WHITE WINE
1/2 tsp. ALLSPICE

Place chicken breasts on dinner plates. In small bowl, combine beans, salsa, wine and allspice. Top each chicken serving with bean mixture. Heat in microwave. Serve hot. Serves 4.

SEDONA

Side Dishes

Spectacular scenery, incredible red rock formations and lush foliage create an unforgettable visual experience.

Green Tamale Casserole

1 pkg. frozen GREEN CORN TAMALES
   (usually 6-8 per package)
1 can (15 oz.) TOMATOES AND GREEN CHILES
2 cups SOUR CREAM
1 1/2 cup CHEDDAR CHEESE, grated

Thaw tamales, remove husks and place in large baking dish. Pour tomatoes and chiles over all. Cover with sour cream and sprinkle cheese over top. Bake in 350 degree oven or microwave on high until cheese is melted.

Serves 6.

Chile Potatoes

4 baking POTATOES, baked in oven or microwave
1/2 cup (1 stick) BUTTER or MARGARINE
2 Tbsp. FLOUR
1 cup LIGHT CREAM or WHOLE MILK
1/2 cup GREEN ONIONS, chopped
1 can (7 oz.) diced GREEN CHILES or 1 JALAPEÑO,
   seeded and diced
1 tsp. GARLIC PEPPER

Place baked potatoes on warmed platter. In large skillet, melt butter, stir in flour until all is absorbed. Slowly add cream and stir to make a thickened white sauce. Add onions, chiles and pepper. Pour thickened sauce in each potato. Serve extra sauce with meal.

Serves 4.

Corn Custard

1 can (12 oz.) whole kernel
   CORN, drained
3 EGGS
1/4 tsp. NUTMEG

2 Tbsp. SUGAR
1/8 tsp. PEPPER
1 cup MILK
1 cup CREAM

This recipe uses canned corn but if fresh corn is available use 8 ears and add 2 tablespoons of extra sugar.

Place corn in large bowl. Beat eggs, add to corn along with remaining ingredients. Stir well. Pour into 8 x 8 buttered baking dish. Place dish into larger dish, fill with water 1 inch deep. Bake in 350 degree oven for 1 hour or until knife inserted into center comes out clean.

Serves 6.

Red Potatoes

2 lbs. POTATOES, cubed
2 Tbsp. crushed RED PEPPERS
1 Tbsp. diced PARSLEY FLAKES
1 tsp. SALT
4 Tbsp. BUTTER

Cook cubed potatoes in water to cover in large sauce-pan until done. Drain potatoes thoroughly. Return to pan. Add remaining ingredients and toss gently to coat potatoes. Serve hot. Wonderful with beef. Use any leftovers chilled as a salad.

Serves 6.

Hot Jalapeño Rice

Sipapu Lodge Bed & Breakfast

2 cups BROWN RICE
2-3 canned JALAPEÑOS, diced
1 Tbsp. JALAPEÑO JUICE
1/2 tsp. CUMIN

SALT, to taste
1/4 cup BUTTER
1 TOMATO, sliced
fresh PARSLEY, chopped

Cook rice according to package directions. Drain and rinse. In large baking dish, combine rice, jalapeños, juice from canned jalapeño, cumin, salt and butter. Heat in microwave or oven until butter is melted. Garnish with tomato slices and parsley. Serve hot.

Serves 6.

 Camp Garden was an early name given Sedona by cavalry from Camp Verde who liked to cool off here in the summer.

Chile Cheese Squash

Squash was one of the earliest crops grown by the first inhabitants of the Sedona area.

1 lb. SQUASH, zucchini, summer or yellow,
    cut in 1/4-inch pieces
1/2 cup MAYONNAISE (not salad dressing)
1 can (4 oz.) diced GREEN CHILES
1/2 cup CHEDDAR CHEESE, grated
1/2 cup BREAD CRUMBS

Cook squash until just tender. Drain well. Return to pan, stir in remaining ingredients. Serve hot.

Serves 4.

Perfect Petite Peas

3 pkgs. frozen petite PEAS   2 Tbsp. OLIVE OIL
1/2 cup ONIONS, diced   8 oz. SOUR CREAM
1 cup canned or fresh MUSHROOMS

Cook peas according to package directions. Drain and set aside. Sauté onions and mushrooms in oil until onions are limp and slightly browned. Stir in peas to heat. Remove from heat, stir in sour cream. Warm slightly, serve at once.

Serves 4.

Tomato Pie

Superb with barbecued meats!

1 PIE SHELL, unbaked
6 lg. TOMATOES, sliced
1/8 tsp. GARLIC PEPPER
1/2 tsp. dried ITALIAN HERBS
1/2 tsp. dried OREGANO LEAVES
1 cup GREEN ONIONS, cut in 1/4 inch pieces
2 cups LONGHORN or CHEDDAR CHEESE, grated
1 cup MAYONNAISE (not salad dressing)
3/4 cup PARMESAN CHEESE, grated

Prick pie shell and bake in 375 degree oven for 10 minutes. Remove from oven and set aside. Cover bottom of shell with 1/2 the tomatoes and 1/2 all other ingredients except parmesan cheese. Repeat layer. Top with all the parmesan cheese. Bake in 350 degree oven for 45 minutes.

Serves 6-8.

Lemon Rice

This is a wonderful dish served with fish or seafood.

2 cups WATER
1/4 cup LEMON JUICE
1/4 cup LIME JUICE
1 Tbsp. grated LEMON RIND
1 cup regular uncooked RICE

Combine water, lemon and lime juice and lemon rind in medium pan. Bring quickly to boil, reduce heat and add rice. Simmer gently, covered, for 30 minutes, until all the liquid is gone.

Serves 4.

Baked Hominy

2 cans (15 oz. ea.) WHITE HOMINY
1 can (7 oz.) diced GREEN CHILES
1 can (10 1/2 oz.) CHEDDAR CHEESE SOUP
1/8 tsp. PEPPER
1 tsp. dried CILANTRO
1 cup SOUR CREAM
1 cup LONGHORN or CHEDDAR CHEESE, grated

Place hominy in colander and rinse well with cold running water. Allow to drain. Preheat oven to 375 degrees. In large bowl, combine drained hominy and all other ingredients except cheese. Place in baking dish and bake for 45 minutes. Remove from oven, sprinkle cheese on top and return to oven until the cheese melts and is bubbly.

Serves 6.

Foul Medammas

(Fava Beans)

La Mediterranée Restaurant. This recipe won grand prize at the Arizona Garlic Festival 1992.

2 cups dry FAVA BEANS
1 tsp. BAKING SODA
1 med. ONION, chopped
2 GARLIC CLOVES, crushed
2 TOMATOES, chopped
juice of 1 LEMON
2 Tbsp. OLIVE OIL
SALT and PEPPER, dash

Soak beans overnight covered with water to which baking soda has been added. Replace with fresh water the next day and boil until beans are tender. Drain, adding remaining ingredients and mix thoroughly until half of the beans are broken.

Serves 4.

 *Two campgrounds in Oak Creek Canyon with interesting names are Banjo Bill Campground (named for banjo player Bill Dwyer who squatted there in 1880) and Bootlegger Campground (named for Bear Howard's grandson Jess, who had stills there, and all up and down the canyon!)*

Cottonwood Stuffing

A deliciously different stuffing
with southwestern flavors.

1 lb. CHORIZO
1 lb. JIMMY DEAN® SAGE SAUSAGE
2 cans (15 oz. ea.) BLACK BEANS, drained
1 lg. WHITE ONION, diced
1/4 tsp. GARLIC POWDER
3 Tbsp. PARSLEY, minced
1 tsp. dried CILANTRO
1 sm. bag TORTILLA CHIPS, unsalted, if available

Cook chorizo and sausage in large skillet until cooked. Drain very well. Saute onions lightly in same pan, return sausages to pan, add beans, garlic powder, parsley and cilantro. Place tortillas in large plastic bag, roll to crush and add to skillet. Simmer all together 20 minutes.

Stuffs 12-pound turkey

Zucchini & Salsa

3 med. ZUCCHINI or other summer SQUASHES, about 1 lb.,
    cut into 1/2-inch pieces
1 cup SALSA

Cook squash until tender yet crisp. Drain very well. Combine squash and salsa. Heat in microwave or in saucepan.

Serves 4.

Fanned Potatoes

6 med. baking POTATOES
1 stick BUTTER or MARGARINE, melted
1 Tbsp. PARSLEY FLAKES
3 Tbsp. PARMESAN CHEESE
PAPRIKA

Slice potatoes to within 1/4 inch of bottom, making slices about 1/4 inch thick. Gently spread to make a fan-shape. Place in baking dish and brush each with melted butter. Bake in 425 degree oven for 1 hour or until done. Sprinkle each with parsley flakes, cheese and paprika and bake another 30 minutes.

Serves 6.

Taco Potatoes

Sipapu Lodge

6 med. POTATOES, with or without peels, cooked
1/2 tsp. each: SALT, CHILI POWDER, CUMIN,
    PAPRIKA, OREGANO and GARLIC POWDER
1 sm. ONION, diced
1/4 cup BUTTER
SOUR CREAM and PARSLEY as garnish

Cut cooked potatoes into bite-sized pieces and place in large baking dish. Combine all other ingredients except sour cream and parsley and pour over potatoes. Heat in oven until heated and butter is melted. Serve with sour cream and parsley as garnish.

Serves 6.

Navajo Fry Bread

To the northeast of Sedona lies the vast Navajo nation. Here is a favorite Navajo staple that can be topped with beans, meats, cheeses and vegetables.

2 cups FLOUR
2 tsp. BAKING POWDER
1 Tbsp. SALT
1/4 cup POWDERED MILK
warm WATER
1 cup VEGETABLE OIL

In large bowl, combine flour, baking powder, salt and milk. Add enough warm water to form soft dough. Knead several times and form into 6 large pancake shapes. Fry, one at a time, in hot oil, turning once.

Makes 6 breads.

 ## *Sedona Films*

The following is a list of some of the movies filmed in their entirety here in Sedona:

Redhead and the Cowboy	*The Rounders*	*Legend of Lobo*
Riders of the Purple Sage	*Shotgun*	*Wild Rovers*
Angel and the Bad Man	*The Wild Rovers*	*Revenge of a Killer*
Sedona Place Names	*Indian Uprising*	*Leave Her to Heaven*
Call of the Canyon	*Flaming Feather*	*Yellowstone Kelly*
Johnny Guitar	*Cimmaron Strip*	*Survival*
Broken Arrow	*Half-Breed*	*Billy the Kid*

SEDONA

Salsas & Sauces

The famous Oak Creek Canyon switchbacks climb the north end of the canyon toward Flagstaff. At the top is a breathtaking view of evergreens and multicolored cliffs in the gorge below.

The West's Best Barbecue Sauce

This sauce has been around for so long that its origin has disappeared into the sunset. Its uses are limited only by the imagination of the chef!

1 cup VEGETABLE OIL
1 1/2 cups WHITE ONION, diced
1 1/2 cups KETCHUP
1 1/2 cups BOTTLED WATER
1/3 cup LEMON JUICE
1/3 cup LIME JUICE
3 Tbsp. WHITE SUGAR
3 Tbsp. BROWN SUGAR
1/3 cup WORCESTERSHIRE SAUCE
3 tsp. prepared MUSTARD
1/2 cup RED WINE VINEGAR
1 Tbsp. CHILI POWDER
1 tsp. dried SWEET BASIL
1 tsp. GARLIC POWDER
1/3 cup PANCAKE SYRUP

Combine all ingredients in large saucepan. Simmer slowly at least 2 hours uncovered. Sauce will become bitter if cooked with a lid.

Makes about 4 cups.

 Sedona, with a permanent population of about 15,000, averages four million visitors per year.

Swedish Mustard

1 cup SUGAR
1/3 cup dry MUSTARD
BOURBON

In small bowl, blend sugar and dry mustard until thoroughly mixed. Add enough bourbon, a few drops at a time, to desired consistency. Store in refrigerator in covered container for 7 days before using. Stir frequently while the mustard is aging.

Cilantro Salsa

Salsa is perhaps the most popular and best known of all southwestern foods and has become a favorite addition to menus everywhere.

4 med. TOMATOES, diced
1 sm. ONION, diced
1 BELL PEPPER, any color, diced
1 can (4 oz.) diced GREEN CHILES, drained
1/2 tsp. dried OREGANO
1/4 tsp. SALT
1/2 cup fresh CILANTRO, or 1 Tbsp. dried cilantro
1 Tbsp. ORANGE JUICE

Combine all ingredients in medium bowl. Serve chilled or at room temperature.

Makes about 2 cups.

All Purpose Salsa

4 cups TOMATOES, chopped
2 Tbsp. diced GREEN CHILES
1 1/2 tsp. LEMON JUICE
1 1/2 tsp. VEGETABLE or OLIVE OIL
1 tsp. dried OREGANO

Combine all the ingredients and mix well. Refrigerate until chilled or eat at room temperature. Makes 1 1/2 cups.

Everyday Salsa

5 lg. TOMATOES, chopped
1/2 bunch CILANTRO, chopped
1/3 cup GREEN ONION, chopped
1 1/2 Tbsp. canned JALAPEÑOS, diced
1 Tbsp. LIME JUICE
SALT and PEPPER to taste

Mix together and refrigerate. Makes 3 cups.

Easy Salsa

1 lg. can (16 oz.) TOMATOES
1 can (4 oz.) diced GREEN CHILES, undrained
1/2 tsp. GARLIC SALT
1/2 tsp. OREGANO
1/2 tsp. dried CILANTRO
1/4 tsp. CHILI POWDER

Mash tomatoes well, add can of chiles. Stir in the spices and herbs, mixing well. This salsa can be stored for several days in the refrigerator. Makes 2 1/2 cups.

Pinto Bean Gravy

*This gravy is delicious served over vegetables or pasta
and is also great served over jalapeño buscuits.*

1 can (15 oz.) PINTO BEANS, undrained
1 Tbsp. instant CHICKEN BOUILLON
1 tsp. dried ONION FLAKES
1/2 cup WATER
1/8 tsp. GARLIC PEPPER

Combine all ingredients in a blender or food processor. When smooth, place in medium saucepan and simmer, stirring frequently until thickened.

Makes about 2 cups or 4 servings.

Sweet & Sour Sauce for Cabbage

1 EGG YOLK	1 tsp. HORSERADISH
1/8 tsp. SALT	2 Tbsp. WHITE VINEGAR
1 Tbsp. SUGAR	1/2 cup SOUR CREAM
1/4 tsp. PAPRIKA	1 small head CABBAGE

Cook cabbage and cut into wedges. In a medium saucepan, combine egg yolk, salt, sugar and paprika. Stir over low heat for 1 minute. Add horseradish, vinegar and sour cream. Stir until slightly thickened. Serve over cabbage or other vegetable of choice.

Makes about 3/4 cups sauce.

Mexican Marinade

1/2 cup VEGETABLE or OLIVE OIL
1 tsp. CHILI POWDER
1/2 tsp. ground PEPPER
1 tsp. dried ITALIAN SEASONING
1/2 tsp. GARLIC POWDER

Combine all ingredients and store in refrigerator. Use as a marinade for meats and vegetables.

Makes about 1/2 cup.

Shrimp Sauce

3/4 lb. cooked SHRIMP, chopped
2 cloves GARLIC, minced
2 Tbsp. OLIVE OIL
1/4 cup PARSLEY, chopped
1 tsp. OREGANO
1 Tbsp. FLOUR
1 cup MILK

In a medium skillet, combine shrimp, garlic and olive oil. Sauté until garlic is lightly browned. Add parsley and oregano. Slowly sprinkle flour over mixture and stir well. Add milk slowly and cook until sauce bubbles and thickens, stirring constantly.

Serve over pasta or rice.

Makes about 2 cups.

SEDONA

Desserts

The diverse red rock formations have inspired many interesting names including Cockscomb, Chimney Rock, Capitol Butte, Sugar Loaf and Coffee Pot Rock.

Coffee Pot Fudge

BUTTER or MARGARINE
3 cups SUGAR
1 cup MILK
1/2 cup CREAM
1 Tbsp. light CORN SYRUP
3 Tbsp. instant COFFEE
3 Tbsp. BUTTER or MARGARINE
1 tsp. VANILLA
1 pkg. (6 oz.) SEMI-SWEET CHOCOLATE BITS
1 cup PECANS, chopped

Butter the bottom and sides of large saucepan. In saucepan, combine sugar, milk, cream, corn syrup and coffee. Cook over medium heat until mixture boils and sugar dissolves, stirring constantly. Cook until small amount forms a soft ball when dropped into cool water. Add butter and let cool until barely warm. Beat until mixture thickens. Add vanilla, chocolate and pecans. Spread in shallow, buttered, 12 x 12 pan. Cut into squares when firm.

Yields 1 pound.

Slide Rock State Park was originally owned by Harrington Fall and known as Fall's Place. Falls built a cabin there. The property was purchased by Frank Pendley in 1907. He improved the grounds and planted orchards.

Castle Rock Rum Balls

A local favorite that uses pecans grown in the Verde Valley.

1 1/2 cups VANILLA WAFERS, crushed
1/4 cup HONEY
2 cups PECANS, ground
1/3 cup DARK RUM
POWDERED SUGAR

In medium bowl, combine all the ingredients except the powdered sugar. Shape by hand into 1-inch balls and roll in the sugar. Store covered in refrigerator.

Makes about 30 rum balls.

Fudge Pie

1/4 lb. BUTTER or MARGARINE
2 squares baking CHOCOLATE
2 EGGS
1 cup SUGAR
1/4 cup FLOUR

Melt butter or margarine in medium saucepan. Add chocolate and stir until melted. Add eggs, sugar and flour. Combine well. Pour into buttered pie pan. Bake in 350 degree oven for 30 minutes. Cool, cut into 6 pieces. This is great served with ice cream and chocolate sauce.

Serves 6.

Lemon Sours

3/4 cup BUTTER or MARGARINE
1/2 cup SUGAR
1 1/2 cups FLOUR
2 EGGS
1/4 tsp. BAKING POWDER
1 cup BROWN SUGAR
1 cup chopped WALNUTS
juice of 1 lg. LEMON
1 tsp. LEMON PEEL
1 Tbsp. BUTTER or MARGARINE
POWDERED SUGAR

Mix in medium bowl the 3/4 cup butter or margarine, sugar and flour. Press into lightly buttered 8 x 8 baking pan. Bake in 325 degree oven for 15 minutes. While this is baking, combine eggs, baking powder, sugar and walnuts in medium bowl. Pour over first mixture and bake again for 20 minutes. In mixing bowl, stir together lemon juice, lemon peel, butter and enough powdered sugar to make a spreading consistency. Spread over hot mixture in pan. Cool completely, cut into squares.

Makes about 32 squares.

 "Soldier's Wash" was a very popular campground for the Camp Verde cavalry.

Baked Bananas

Cozy Cactus Bed & Breakfast Inn

6 BANANAS, peeled
1/3 cup BUTTER, melted
3 Tbsp. LEMON JUICE
1/3 cup BROWN SUGAR

1 tsp. CINNAMON
1 cup COCONUT, grated
1 cup WALNUTS, chopped

Place bananas in large baking dish. Combine butter, lemon juice, sugar, cinnamon, coconut and walnuts. Distribute evenly over the bananas, turning them to thoroughly coat each banana. Bake in 375 degree oven for 20 minutes, turning once after 10 minutes. Serve warm.

Serves 6.

Chocolate Cheesecake

Mexico's greatest culinary gift to the world is chocolate, which was introduced to the rest of the world in the early sixteenth century.

1 pkg. CHOCOLATE CAKE MIX
4 EGGS
1/3 cup BUTTER, softened
1 pkg. (16 oz.) CREAM CHEESE, softened
2 tsp. VANILLA EXTRACT
3/4 cup SUGAR

In large bowl, combine cake mix, butter and 1 egg. Pour into 9 x 13 baking pan. Beat cream cheese, eggs, vanilla and sugar until smooth. Spread over cake mix. Bake in 350 degree oven for 25-30 minutes. Frost if desired. Chill at least 12 hours before slicing.

Baked Stuffed Pears

Cozy Cactus Bed & Breakfast Inn

4 PEARS
1/4 cup RAISINS
3 Tbsp. WALNUTS, chopped
2 1/2 Tbsp. SUGAR
1 Tbsp. LEMON JUICE
1/4 cup warm WATER
1/4 cup LIGHT CORN SYRUP

Peel pears, leaving stems on. Core pears from the bottom. In small bowl, combine raisins, walnuts, sugar and lemon juice. Fill the cavity of each pear with the mixture, equally divided. Place stuffed pears upright in a deep baking dish. Combine water and corn syrup and pour over pears. Cover and bake in 350 degree oven for 1 hour 15 minutes. Serve warm.

Serves 4.

Tuzigoot ruins, 2 miles northwest of Cottonwood was inhabited by the Sinagua Indians. There you can see the remains of their masonry houses on the mesa tops and in caves. The visitor center and museum are open every day of the year.

Lime Cookies

Citrus grows in many areas of the Southwest as a major commercial crop. These cookies can be made with any combination of citrus.

1 cup BUTTER, softened
1/2 cup LIGHT BROWN SUGAR
1/2 cup WHITE SUGAR
1 EGG
1/4 tsp. BAKING SODA
2 Tbsp. fresh LIME JUICE
1 Tbsp. grated LIME RIND
1 1/2 cups FLOUR
1/2 cup PECANS or WALNUTS, diced

Cream together butter and both sugars. Add egg, beat well. Add remaining ingredients and blend until smooth. Chill 1 hour. Drop by the teaspoonful on ungreased cookie sheet. Bake in 375 degree oven for 8-10 minutes. Cookies should be slightly browned at the edges. Allow to cool at least 1 1/2 hours.

Makes about 3 dozen cookies.

 Elmerville, near Red Rock Crossing, was formerly called Jackass Flat because of the wild burros that once roamed the area.

Flan

Flan is Mexico's most famous dessert. It has become a favorite everywhere.

1 cup WHITE SUGAR
1 can SWEETENED CONDENSED MILK
1 1/2 cups HEAVY CREAM
1/2 tsp. ground CINNAMON
4 EGGS

Heat sugar in skillet over medium high heat. When sugar begins to melt, lower heat and stir until sugar is melted. Pour into a 1 quart baking dish, rotating to coat the sides. In medium bowl, combine milk, cream, cinnamon and eggs. Pour mixture over sugar. Place baking dish in pan of hot water so that water comes halfway up the sides of the baking dish. Bake in 325 degree oven for 1 hour 45 minutes or until knife inserted in center comes out clean.

Serves 6-8.

Tlaquepaque (Te-la-kee-pa-kee) Village houses many art galleries and gift shops. Its Spanish Colonial design features many fountains, sculptures and flowered courtyards.

Fresh Apple Cake

*Small apple orchards dot the flanks of Oak Creek and
the Verde River throughout the Sedona region.*

2 EGGS
2 cups SUGAR
3 cups FLOUR, sifted
1 tsp. BAKING SODA
1/2 tsp. SALT
1/2 tsp. ground CINNAMON
1 1/2 cup VEGETABLE OIL
2 tsp. VANILLA EXTRACT
1 1/2 cups WALNUTS, chopped
3 cups APPLES, peeled and chopped

Beat eggs and sugar together in large bowl. Add
sifted flour, soda, salt and cinnamon. Stir well. Add
remaining ingredients. Pour into 9 x 13 baking dish.
Bake in 300 degree oven for 1 1/2 hours. Top with
whipped cream or the following *Rum Sauce*.

Rum Sauce

1/2 cup BUTTER   **1 EGG, beaten**
1 cup SUGAR   **4 Tbsp. DARK RUM**
1 cup HOT WATER

In a medium saucepan, cream butter and sugar together. Gradually stir in hot water and boil gently until
the mixture is slightly thickened. Add egg and beat
mixture well. Remove from heat, stir in rum. Serve warm
over slices of cake or split muffins.

Makes 1 1/2 cups sauce.

Desert Dream Bars

1/2 cup BUTTER or MARGARINE, softened	1 cup COCONUT 1 cup PECANS
1/2 cup BROWN SUGAR	2 Tbsp. FLOUR
1 cup FLOUR	1/4 tsp. SALT
2 EGGS	1/2 tsp. BAKING POWDER
1 cup BROWN SUGAR	1 tsp. VANILLA EXTRACT

In medium bowl, mix butter, sugar and flour. Press into greased 9 x 13 baking pan. Bake in 350 degree oven for 15 minutes. In large bowl, combine remaining ingredients and spread over baked first mixture. Bake another 25-30 minutes. Cut into bars while still warm.

Red Rock Christmas Cake

1 cup BUTTER, softened
2 1/2 cups SUGAR
1 1/2 tsp. ALMOND EXTRACT
8 EGGS
4 cups FLOUR
1 pkg. (16 oz.) RAISINS
2 jars (8 oz. each) CANDIED CHERRIES
1 jar (8 oz.) CANDIED CITRON, chopped

In large bowl, beat butter, sugar and extract together. Add eggs, 2 at a time, beat in flour. Add raisins, cherries and citron. Bake in 300 degree oven in well greased tube or bundt pan for 2 1/2 hours. Let cool 30 minutes.

Spice Cake with Beer

This delicious cake was inspired by the many excellent breweries and wineries existing throughout Arizona.

1/2 cup SHORTENING
1/2 cup WHITE SUGAR
1/2 cup BROWN SUGAR
2 EGGS
2 cups FLOUR
2 tsp. BAKING POWDER
1/2 tsp. BAKING SODA

1/4 tsp. SALT
1/2 tsp. CLOVES
1/2 tsp. ALLSPICE
1/4 tsp. ground NUTMEG
1 tsp. ground CINNAMON
1 1/4 cups BEER

In large bowl, cream together shortening, both sugars and eggs. Add remaining ingredients. Beat well. Pour into well-greased 9 x 13 baking pan. Bake in 350 degree oven for 45-60 minutes.

Buttermilk Pie

1/2 cup BUTTER
2 cups SUGAR
4 Tbsp. FLOUR
3 EGGS, beaten
1 1/2 cups BUTTERMILK
1 tsp. VANILLA or RUM EXTRACT
grated NUTMEG to taste
9-inch unbaked PIE SHELL

Cream butter and sugar together, add flour and eggs, beat well. Stir in buttermilk, extract and nutmeg. Bake in 350 degree oven for 1 hour or until knife inserted in center of pie comes out clean. Cool completely and chill in refrigerator.

Zucchini Cake

In Sedona's ideal climate, vegetable gardens
are very popular. The common squash, zucchini, grows
well in containers and gardens.

3 cups ZUCCHINI SQUASH, grated
1 1/2 cups VEGETABLE OIL
3 cups SUGAR
4 EGGS
2 tsp. VANILLA EXTRACT
3 cups FLOUR
1 1/2 tsp. BAKING SODA
1 1/2 tsp. BAKING POWDER
1 1/2 tsp. CINNAMON
1 cup RAISINS
1 cup WALNUTS, chopped

In large bowl, mix zucchini, oil, sugar, eggs and vanilla. In medium bowl, mix flour, baking powder and soda, cinnamon, raisins and walnuts. Combine mixtures well. Bake in 9 x 13 baking pan in 350 degree oven for 1 hour.

 Birds that may be found in the Sedona area include:
- *Kingfisher*
- *Green Violet Swallow*
- *White Throated Swift*
- *Blue Grossbeak*
- *Western Tanager*
- *Yellow Warbler*
- *Stellar Jay*
- *Water Ouzel*

Mexican Wedding Cakes

A traditional Mexican dessert. Sedona pecans freeze well making them available all year long for use in these delicious little cakes.

2 1/2 cups FLOUR
1/2 tsp. ground CINNAMON
1 cup BUTTER, softened
1 cup PECANS, diced fine
1/2 cup POWDERED SUGAR
1 1/2 tsp. VANILLA EXTRACT
POWDERED SUGAR

In large bowl, combine flour and cinnamon. Add butter, pecans, powdered sugar and vanilla. Stir well. Using your hands, shape into 1-inch balls. Bake on an ungreased baking sheet in 400 degree oven for 10-12 minutes. Roll in powdered sugar when removed from oven. When cool, roll in powdered sugar again. Makes about 4 dozen cakes.

 Animals that may be found in the Sedona area include:

- *Gray squirrel*
- *Abert squirrel*
- *Mule deer*
- *Mountain lion*
- *Coyote*
- *Bobcat*

- *Skunk*
- *Raccoon*
- *Porcupine*
- *Gray fox*
- *Chipmunk*

Walnut Sour Cream Cake

*Walnuts and pecans grow very well in the Arizona
deserts and make lovely shade trees. Recipes are
more fun to make when at least some of
the ingredients are homegrown!*

1/2 lb. (2 sticks) BUTTER or MARGARINE
1 cup SUGAR
2 EGGS, beaten
2 cups FLOUR
1 tsp. BAKING SODA
1/2 tsp. SALT
1 cup SOUR CREAM
1 tsp. VANILLA EXTRACT

Cream butter and sugar together. Add eggs, then
remaining ingredients. Pour 1/2 batter into 9-inch buttered baking dish. Prepare filling and topping as follows:

Walnut Filling & Topping

1/3 cup BROWN SUGAR
1/4 cup WHITE SUGAR
1 tsp. CINNAMON
1 cup WALNUTS, chopped

Mix sugars, cinnamon and walnuts in medium bowl.
Cover batter with 1/2 the walnut mixture, add remaining
batter and top with remaining walnut mixture. Bake in
350 degree oven for 40-45 minutes.

Pumpkin Bread

Cozy Cactus Bed & Breakfast Inn

1 1/2 cups SUGAR
2 EGGS
1/2 cup VEGETABLE OIL
1 1/2 cups mashed PUMPKIN (canned or fresh)
1 2/3 cups FLOUR
1 tsp. BAKING SODA
1 1/2 tsp. BAKING POWDER
3/4 tsp. SALT
1 tsp. NUTMEG
1 tsp. CINNAMON
1 tsp. CLOVES

Combine sugar, eggs, oil and pumpkin. Sift together flour, soda, baking powder, salt, nutmeg, cinnamon and cloves. Combine mixtures, beat by hand. Grease and flour 3 small or 1 regular loaf pan. Bake in 325 degree oven for 70 minutes.

Exactly 5 miles northeast on SR179 from the bridge near Tlaquepaque is an unusual formation called Merry-go-round Rock. This was the locale for a key scene in the 1950 film "Broken Arrow" which stared Jeff Chandler as Apache Chief Cochise.

Lemon-Poppy Seed Bread

Cozy Cactus Bed & Breakfast Inn

3 cups FLOUR
3/4 cup SUGAR
1/2 tsp. SALT
1/2 cup POPPY SEEDS
3 1/2 tsp. BAKING POWDER
1 1/2 cups LOW-FAT MILK
2 lg. EGGS
1/4 cup CANOLA OIL
1 LEMON, rind and juice, with rind grated

Combine flour, sugar, salt, poppy seeds and baking powder in large bowl. In medium bowl, combine milk, eggs, oil and lemon. Combine 2 mixtures, stirring well until smooth. Pour into greased loaf pan. Bake in 350 degree oven for 1 hour. Cool 10 minutes, turn out on wire rack. Wrap in foil and store overnight before slicing.

There are many exciting ways to see Sedona such as balloon expeditions, helicopter rides, jeep tours and on horseback.

Apricot-Banana Bread

The Graham Bed and Breakfast Inn

2 cups FLOUR
1 tsp. BAKING POWDER
1/2 tsp. SALT
1 cup SUGAR
1/2 cup dried APRICOTS, chopped
1/2 cup WALNUTS, chopped
3/4 cup ripe BANANA, mashed
1/2 cup MILK
1 EGG
1/4 cup BUTTER or MARGARINE, melted

In large bowl, mix flour, baking powder, baking soda, salt and sugar. Stir in chopped apricots and nuts, mixing until well coated. In separate bowl, combine banana, milk, egg and butter. Stir banana mixture into dry ingredients just until all are well-blended. Grease 3 small (3 x 5 1/2) pans or 1 regular bread loaf pan. Pour in batter which will be fairly stiff. Bake in preheated oven at 350 degrees for 45 minutes or until bread begins to shrink from the sides of the pans. Let bread cool 10 minutes, turn out on rack to cool.

Note: Freezes well. Try this bread with whipped honey butter!

 Red Rock State Park has beautiful hiking trails along Oak Creek.

SEDONA

Beverages

Bell Rock and Courthouse Butte offer great hiking trails and the added attraction of being one of the famous "vortex" locations.

Margaritas

*The margarita is a classic favorite of the Southwest.
They are traditionally served in salt-rimmed cocktail
glasses. To prepare the glasses, rub the rims with
lemon or lime juice and dip into salt.
Chill until serving time.*

1 1/2 cups TEQUILA
1 1/2 cups LIME JUICE
1 cup TRIPLE SEC
2 cups crushed ICE
6 LIME SLICES

Combine tequila, juice, triple sec and ice in shaker.
Shake well. Pour into 6 salt-rimmed glasses and add lime
slice to each.

Serves 6.

Coffee Pot Tea

*Tennis is a popular activity in the Sedona area. This
tea will keep at room temperature all day and is ideal
for sipping at courtside.*

To make tea, use a regular coffee maker using 2 filters
instead of 1 as for coffee. For a 10-12 cup coffeepot, place
8 tablespoons of loose tea in the filter. Add a full pot of
bottled water and brew.

Serve tea over crushed ice or ice cubes.

Strawberry Tequila

fresh STRAWBERRIES, halved
TEQUILA

Fill a quart jar with fresh strawberries. Pour tequila over strawberries until jar is filled. Cover tightly and store in dark closet for two weeks. Strain and serve as a liqueur.

Note: This delightful liqueur can be made with any fresh berries.

Oak Creek Canyon ranges from 1500 to 2500 feet deep and averages one mile from rim to rim. The canyon is 12 miles long.

After Dinner Kahlua

1 pt. VANILLA ICE CREAM, softened
1/2 cup KAHLUA®
1 cup black COFFEE

Place all ingredients in a blender and mix well. Serve in mugs.

Serves 4.

Spiced Coffee

This is also delicious served over ice.

4 cups bottled WATER
1/3 cup dark BROWN SUGAR
1/2 cup instant COFFEE
4 CINNAMON STICKS

Combine water and sugar in medium saucepan. Bring to a boil and stir until sugar is dissolved. Reduce heat to simmer, stir in coffee and simmer 1-2 minutes. Pour into mugs, add cinnamon sticks.

Serves 4.

 The Sedona Arts Center provides a variety of musical and artistic events throughout the year.

Tequila Sunrise

1 1/3 cups ORANGE JUICE
1/4 cup LIME JUICE
1/2 cup TEQUILA
2 1/2 Tbsp. GRENADINE

Combine orange and lime juices with tequila. Pour into 3 ice-filled glasses. Slowly add grenadine in equal amounts to each glass.

Serves 3.

Strawberries Kahlua

Kahlua is a drink that is delicious and versatile. This is a local favorite using Sedona's superb strawberries.

3 cups fresh STRAWBERRIES, hulled
1 cup WHIPPING CREAM
1/4 cup KAHLUA®

Combine all the ingredients and chill well. Serve in sherbet cups.

Serves 4.

Coffee Liqueur

4 cups SUGAR
1/2 cup instant COFFEE
3 cups BOTTLED WATER (preferably distilled)
1/4 tsp. SALT
2 1/2 cups 80 proof VODKA
3 Tbsp. VANILLA EXTRACT

In large saucepan, stir sugar and coffee together. Add water and salt, place over high heat, stirring constantly until sugar is dissolved. Reduce heat, simmer for 1 hour. Remove from heat, stir in vodka and vanilla. Let cool. Store in tightly covered container.

Makes 1 1/2 quarts.

Note: In addition to being served as a liqueur, this also makes a great topping for ice cream and fruit compote.

Bloody Maria's

2 1/2 cups TOMATO JUICE
2 cans (12 oz. each) V-8® JUICE
3/4 cup LIME JUICE
1 Tbsp. WORCESTERSHIRE SAUCE
1/2 tsp. TABASCO® SAUCE
1 tsp. CELERY SALT
VODKA

Combine and blend on low speed in blender. Chill well. When ready to serve, add 1 part vodka for every 2 parts mix.

Serves 8-10.

 Manzanita Forest Camp is the only site of a mining claim ever filed in Oak Creek Canyon.

Canyon Mist

8 scoops VANILLA ICE CREAM
3 Tbsp. CREME DE MENTHE
2 Tbsp. BRANDY
3 Tbsp. TRIPLE SEC

Place all ingredients in blender and blend on lowest speed. Serve in mugs.

Serves 4.

Cafe de Olla

Mexico is famous for its exceptional coffee. This is a widely used addition to many recipes.

4 cups strong brewed COFFEE
3 cups LIGHT CREAM
1/3 cup BRANDY
1/3 cup RUM
1/3 cup CREME DE CACAO

Simmer together in large pan, preferably earthenware. DO NOT BOIL.

Serves 6.

 Honanki and Palatki are the two largest cliff dwellings in the area. They are believed to have been constructed 700 years ago.

Sangria

Sangria is a favorite drink throughout the Southwest.

2 bottles (750 ML) dry red or rosé WINE
1 cup SUGAR
2 ORANGES, sliced very thin
1 LEMON, sliced very thin
1 LIME, sliced very thin
2 bottles (10 oz. ea.) CLUB SODA

Combine all ingredients and chill well. Serve in tall glasses over ice.

Makes 2 quarts.

Mexican Martinis

1 cup very dry VERMOUTH
4 cups GIN or VODKA
12 ICE CUBES
pickled JALAPEÑOS

Place vermouth, gin or vodka and ice in a cocktail shaker. Shake well to chill. Strain into martini glasses. Add jalapeño, on a toothpick, to each glass.

Makes 6 cocktails.

 Hot air balloon rides are offered daily to those who wish a "birds eye" view of this beautiful red rock country.

Tequila Slush

1 1/2 cups TEQUILA
1 can (6 oz.) frozen LIMEADE
1 cup ORANGE JUICE
1 cup crushed ICE (or about 10-12 ice cubes)

Place in blender and blend on high until mixed and slushy.

Serves 4.

Index

About the Author

Susan K. Bollin is a geologist and an author. She has written extensively in the fields of earth science and environmental science for both adults and children. In addition, she has written books for dog, cat and horse owners. Most recently, Ms. Bollin has written cookbooks about southwestern and Mexican foods. In addition to *Sedona Cook Book*, she is also the author of *Salsa Lovers Cook Book*, *Chip and Dip Lovers Cook Book* and *Quick-n-Easy Mexican Recipes*. She and her family live in Arizona.

About the Artist

Kris Steele grew up in Phoenix, Arizona, and began her early college training at Phoenix College and Arizona State University.

After working with Paul Coze, a well-known artist/muralist from France, she studied at the Kansas City Art Institute. She then moved to Los Angeles where she worked with design firms.

Kris has produced many fine art pieces, murals and illustrated cover works for books, illustrated maps and promotions and has a deep love for ceramics. An avid gardener and nature enthusiast, she and her husband are living, working and raising two children in Camp Verde, Arizona.

SALSA LOVERS COOK BOOK

More than 180 taste-tempting recipes for salsas that will make every meal a special event! Salsas for salads, appetizers, main dishes, and desserts! Put some salsa in your life! By Susan K. Bollin.

5 1/2 x 8 1/2—128 pages . . . $5.95

QUICK-N-EASY MEXICAN RECIPES

More than 175 favorite Mexican recipes you can prepare in less than thirty minutes. Traditional items such as tacos, tostadas and enchiladas. Also features easy recipes for salads, soups, breads, desserts and drinks. By Susan K. Bollin.

5 1/2 x 8 1/2—128 pages . . . $5.95

CHIP & DIP LOVERS COOK BOOK

More than 150 recipes for fun and festive dips. Make southwestern dips, dips with fruits and vegetables, meats, poultry and seafood. Salsa dips and dips for desserts. Includes recipes for making homemade chips. By Susan K. Bollin.

5 1/2 x 8 1/2—112 pages . . . $5.95

THE TEQUILA COOK BOOK

Taste the spirit and flavor of the southwest! More than 150 recipes featuring tequila as an ingredient. Wonderful appetizers, soups, salads, main dishes, breads, desserts, and, of course, drinks. Includes fascinating tequila trivia. Truly a unique cook book and a great gift item! By Lynn Nusom.

5 1/2 x 8 1/2—128 pages . . . $7.95

CHILI-LOVERS' COOK BOOK

Chili cookoff prize-winning recipes and regional favorites! The best of chili cookery, from mild to fiery, with and without beans. Plus a variety of taste-tempting foods made with chile peppers. 150,000 copies in print! By Al and Mildred Fischer.

5 1/2 x 8 1/2—128 pages . . . $5.95

ORDER BLANK

GOLDEN WEST PUBLISHERS

☼ 4113 N. Longview Ave. • Phoenix, AZ 85014

602-265-4392 • **1-800-658-5830** • FAX 602-279-6901

Qty	Title	Price	Amount
	Apple-Lovers' Cook Book	6.95	
	Arizona Cook Book	5.95	
	Arizona Small Game & Fish Recipes	5.95	
	Best Barbecue Recipes	5.95	
	Chili-Lovers' Cook Book	5.95	
	Chip and Dip Lovers Cook Book	5.95	
	Christmas in Arizona Cook Book	8.95	
	Citrus Lovers Cook Book	6.95	
	Cowboy Cartoon Cook Book	5.95	
	Date Recipes	6.95	
	Favorite Pumpkin Recipes	6.95	
	New Mexico Cook Book	5.95	
	Pecan-Lovers' Cook Book	6.95	
	Quick-n-Easy Mexican Recipes	5.95	
	Salsa Lovers Cook Book	5.95	
	Sedona Cook Book	7.95	
	Tailgate Fever Cookbook	9.95	
	Tequila Cook Book	7.95	
	What's Cookin' in Arizona	9.95	
Add $2.00 to total order for shipping & handling			$2.00

☐ My Check or Money Order Enclosed. . . . . $ _____

☐ MasterCard   ☐ VISA

Acct. No.   Exp. Date

Signature

Name   Telephone

Address

City/State/Zip

Call for FREE catalog

MasterCard and VISA Orders Accepted ($20 Minimum)

7/94

Sedona

This order blank may be photo-copied.